Stand Up, Struggle Forward

*New Afrikan Revolutionary Writings
on Nation, Class and Patriarchy*

by Sanyika Shakur

KERSPLEBEDEB
2013

Stand Up, Struggle Forward
New Afrikan Revolutionary Writings on Nation, Class and Patriarchy
by Sanyika Shakur

ISBN: 978-1-894946-46-9

Kersplebedeb Publishing and Distribution
CP 63560
CCCP Van Horne
Montreal, Quebec
Canada H3W 3H8

email: info@kersplebedeb.com
web: www.kersplebedeb.com
           www.leftwingbooks.net

Copies available from AK Press:

AK Press
674-A 23rd St.
Oakland, CA
94612

phone: (510) 208-1700
email: info@akpress.org
web: akpress.org

Layout by Kersplebedeb

Printed in Canada

For Nehanda Abiodun, Susan Rosenberg, Assata Shakur,
Silvia Baraldini, Butch Lee, Aminata Umoja,
and the Revolutionary Legacies
of Safiya Bukhari and Marilyn Buck

Asante Sana!

Table of Contents

Foreword

They think they don't need ideology, strategy or tactics.
They think being a warrior is quite enough. And yet, with-
out discipline or direction, they'll end up washing cars, or
unclaimed bodies in the city-state's morgue.

Comrad George Jackson

Power is not the ability to hold a rally, or proclaim broad
sweeping overviews that may or may not have political
utility, but to "define phenomenon and make it act in a de-
sired fashion." This is where power begins—to determine
what goes down on the streets one must organize where
people are at.

Dhoruba Bin-Wahad

It was over 20 years ago that the book *Monster: The Autobiography of an L.A. Gang Member* exploded on the scene and gave us all a front row seat to explore the genocidal brutality of the neo-colonial world of gangbanging. A world that exists at the expense of New Afrikan communities and New Afrikan youth in particular, through our social savage way of attempting to gain power through AK's, bats and beat downs.

Many of us were amazed by the brutality conveyed in this book; others of us related to it. It expressed the social, political, educational, environmental and economic violence that New Afrikans experience daily, only to be reported through mass media as Black-on-Black violence. Through the eyes and soul of a colonial victim we were educated to the dehumanizing of New Afrikans surviving amerikkkan oppression, being reduced to genocidal soldiers and then ultimately caged for our aggression.

But it was in the belly of the beast (prison) that "Monster" underwent a revolutionary transformation, dissecting and re-building himself from the inside out, slaying the colonial thug "Monster" and emerging through a re-birth as "Sanyika Shakur," a New Afrikan Revolutionary Nationalist.

See these collections of "Sanyika" writings capture him at his best, fighting in the belly of the beast, his pen is his "AK 47" shooting through the colonial and neo-colonial oppression. The paper is the razor blade cutting through our warped minds and educating us to have an "overstanding" instead of continuing to have an "understanding" of what must be done. That we must seize power through transforming ourselves, by engaging in "study and struggle"—anything less than that would be social suicide.

Unfortunately, in the present day and time many so-called activists don't want to study, and if they do it is only to roman-ticize themselves and hijack history, talking and organizing as if this is the '60s and '70s... Flawed theories lead to flawed prac-tices! We need individuals who desperately want to be leaders, to be educated. Our communities are suffering on such oppressive levels that any person who provides an act of relief towards their suffering is embraced as a community activist/leader. That is dan-gerous, because now our communities become dependent upon individuals who weren't qualified in the first place. An activist is someone that is actively involved in their community, not some-one who's looking for a photo opportunity, not someone that's looking to be on the news, not someone who's looking to protest just to protest—but someone who's making a difference in their community through improving the quality of the environment and the people.

If you are an activist in your community, you need to be part of the fabric of your community. Not someone that's imported from somewhere else. This is Sanyika's greatest asset to us, his ability to educate, challenge and inform us because every nation needs a theoretician and he learned from the best, "James Yaki Sayles."

These writings are our current New Afrikan revolutionary bible challenging us to be New Afrikans, fight and liberate New Afrikans and ultimately free the land for New Afrikans. This book may disappoint many who are looking for a "gangsta story," but this book is "revolutionary theory" at its finest, and if you read long enough it will possibly transform you into a revolutionary. This book buries "Monster" with the colonial enemy and resurrects "Sanyika," fulfilling his destiny of being a theoretical unifier of the New Afrikan people. Revolutionary theory plus revolutionary practice equals a revolutionary war, which is why it is necessary for us to study and struggle because it is our time to seize the time.

Study, Struggle & Resist

Yusef "Bunchy" Shakur
www.yusefshakur.org
Black August 11, 2013

Our Story
by Santu

I asked my mama one day, I said "mama, if you don't believe in
jesus christ you going to hell right?"

She said "you sholl right honey the good pastor said that the
other night"

"And don't that song say, i was lost but now i'm found, blind but
now i see?"

She said "you sholl right honey, i got it playing on my mp3."

"Well mama is it safe to say that Malcolm X was blind, lost and
going to hell

Because Islam is truly where his heart dwelled?" she hesitated.

"We don't know what Malcolm went through in his final hour

all we can do is pray and hope that he accepted jesus christ as
his lord and savior,

but if he didn't

down with the devil is where he'll serve his penance"

That got me thinking, A man who dedicated his life to continual
liberation of oppressed

people must spend the rest of eternity in hell with other non-
believing people?

i mean, he didn't drink, he didn't smoke, he didn't sleep around
sista so & so husband like some of you church folk,

he didn't lie he didn't steal, would have thought this light-
skinned brother was from the house but this brother was
from the field,

where it's real.

every time i heard him speak everything he said was the truth,

like when JFK died it was just a case of the chickens coming
home to roost.

but still, if you don't believe in jesus christ you're going to hell.

but i was taught that you were judged by your walk not your talk,

by your art not your chalk,

but you mean to tell me if i don't believe in jesus christ i'm going
to hell and it's my fault,

So how did you become a christian?

you see some of y'all were made christians while you were still
diaper pissing,

before you could count to two or make your own decision

let alone even spell religion, y'all know i ain't kidding.

so who is to blame?

is it your mama or the white man who gave your great great
    great grandfather his last name,

oh mama ain't tell you that huh, mama ain't tell you that we had
    our own god before we had to change,

mama ain't tell you how they used to beat the shit out of us if
    we got caught praying to another name,

different from jesus christ, the blonde haired blue eyed man,

mama ain't tell you how our captivity was justified through that
    good book of yours,

"you are to be servants of god's servants" so these are more than
    just chores,

so when you get through reprimanding them field niggas, nigga
    come mop the floor,

but you see that was his story, this is Ours,

We sprung up from the Nile on prosperous land,

highly melinated the Ethiopian translates into the black land,

or should i say the land of the black, it didn't matter cause
    everywhere you looked was black,

fast forward now we talking about the Moors,

the inventors of chess the ones with knowledge galore, this ain't
    no folklore,

but they won't tell you that in his story so ima tell it in Ours.

yeah we believe in the trinity and that's Isis, Osiris and Horus,

Knowledge, Wisdom and Overstanding,

inextricably bound all equally demanding,

we gave thanks to mother earth,

we didn't put tanks on mother earth,

we believed in the barter system there was no need for banks on
mother earth.

then come these savages from out the caves,

would of thought we were child rearing the way we had to teach
them how to behave,

we could've made y'all slaves, but instead knowledge is what we
gave,

tried to teach you how to move with the music,

but all y'all wanted to do was rave, lets turn the page,

2013 Black folks say look how far we've come,

but how far have we come if we in last place but we started the
race number one.

You see Malcolm had a philosophy that was simple and plain:
Know thy self,

Spread thy wealth, The first law of nature is self-preservation so

Protect thy self, By Any Means Necessary!

Stand Up, Struggle Forward

FREE RANGE PREDATORS

Hellfire missiles
From remote-controlled drones,
Spy-techs collect convo's
From the cellphones,
Data banks are bulgin'
To control the zones,
Reactionary agents with the ruse
Of immigration
Subjugate the nations
With neo-colonization,
Productive forces paralyzed
As capital is restructured,
Oppressive apparatus of the State
Promotes bloodsuckers,
Free range predators
Eatin' off of every plate,
IMF consolidated
Church, bank & the State,
Educated fools,
A New World out of Order,
Where corporations make the State
Wage wars & paint borders,
Halliburton, Xe
Kellogg, Brown & Rooth,
Independent contractors
Robots in steel boots,
NASDAQ hegemony

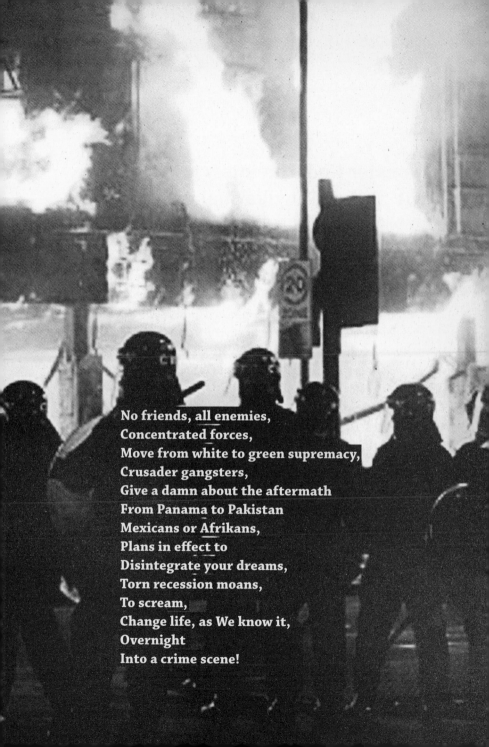

No friends, all enemies,
Concentrated forces,
Move from white to green supremacy,
Crusader gangsters,
Give a damn about the aftermath
From Panama to Pakistan
Mexicans or Afrikans,
Plans in effect to
Disintegrate your dreams,
Torn recession moans,
To scream,
Change life, as We know it,
Overnight
Into a crime scene!

Monster Kody: an interview wit' author Sanyika Shakur
by Minister of Information JR

The first book that I read on my book list after I decided to consciously educate myself to be a part of the movement was Sanyika Shakur's <u>Monster</u> in the mid-'90s. I related to the book, not because I come from street-tribal society of Los Angeles, but because a lot of what he wrote about reminded me of my memories and what I heard about Oakland in the '80s.

A year or two later, reading through a rap magazine, I saw Sanyika's columns, which turned out to be monthly. I was inspired by the sharpness of his ideas, his vocabulary and his grasp on history. I respected the reason he was writing, in the same way that I respected the intellect of Tupac Shakur, another thinker from my generation. I knew that one day I wanted to be able to express myself as articulately as the two of them.

It was an honor for me to get a letter from Sanyika Shakur over the summer of '11 and be able to do this interview with a souljah in this struggle that I highly respect and that I had gained from without ever meeting.

M.O.I. JR

M.O.I. JR: When you were in the streets gang bangin', what brought you into political consciousness?

SANYIKA SHAKUR: Well, first of all, before i even go into answering that, i want to give a clenched fisted salute to you as the minister of information (formerly) for the Prisoners of Conscience Committee. You are doing a beautiful job of getting the requisite information out to the people in order to raise consciousness. We all appreciate your work, Brotha.

Yeah, well, when i was a criminal movin' with the street organization, i had a nascent overstanding about us being essentially one people. i didn't overstand "nation" then, but i overstood that We were a distinct people. See, i started bangin' in the mid-'70s, so the vapors or the residue of the Black Liberation Movement were still palpable. There was still a consciousness there, dig?

And i'm not trying to romanticize it or anything, but We thought We were like the Panthers; i mean that in the sense that

We were outlaws. And again, i'm speaking of having a real rudimentary overstanding of politics, as perceived from the mentality of an adolescent.

i was 11 when i was sponsored in. To me, it was a "Black organization," dig? And We were armed. Of course We, unlike the Panthers, were criminals and parasites. Though as a youth, not knowing the particulars, it wasn't no difference.

We were in what George called the "riot stage" of rebellion. Our resistance was lateral within our own class and nation, as opposed to vertically, up against the oppression that held us down. In this way—well, because our activity was detrimental to ourselves, our community and nation—We were allowed to prosper and in some cases encouraged by the pigs. Consciousness, real, political and revolutionary consciousness, came to me much later and in increments over a span of years.

M.O.I. JR: What were some of the books you studied?

SANYIKA: When i first came to the kamps in 1985, i couldn't really read, perhaps on a fifth grade level. i had no real comprehension. And certainly i couldn't write. See, i need to explain this: In the subculture of bangin', it wasn't about being literate or articulate, and it wasn't about books or academia. It was about action—war—about being physical and macho, dig?

So once i found myself in the hole at San Quentin in 1986, i was stuck because here i was this OG dude, you know, with major street clout and a growing prison rep, but i couldn't read, comprehend or write. So i had to face that, had to confront that, and either go around, you know, or deny it. Or challenge it and resolve it.

And luckily for me, i had cats around me who were interested in growth and development, on an intellectual level. Oh, don't get me wrong, i tried to buffalo my way through at first. i tried to fake it, but the Brothas wasn't letting me off the hook that easy.

So, once i got my reading and comprehension up to par, i started reading what was on the tier—books that were in circulation. i had no funds to order my own books, so i had to read what was available. This was the staple material—*Soledad Brother*, *Blood in My Eye*, *Wretched of the Earth*—and there was the *Burning Spear* newspaper of the African Socialist Party.

But let me say this, i didn't really know how to study at that time. i was reading the material and emotionally attaching myself to what i could overstand. i hadn't yet fully overstood the extent to which i'd need to go in order to transform my criminal, colonial mentality into a revolutionary mentality, dig? That's a serious point there, because without knowing the extent to which you are contaminated by criminality and colonialism, one will not overstand the extent of struggle required to cleanse, dig?

At that stage, in '86 in San Quentin, i just thought revolution was physical violence. i thought We'd only need to gather enough people together in order to get free. i had an ill notion about what We were trying to get free from, and, further, to get free to? That is, i didn't truly overstand capitalism, imperialism or colonialism. Nor did i overstand self-determination or socialism. i thought We were fighting against racism. i didn't begin to overstand what was really going on until i learned how to study and then attained the material that corresponded with my reality.

M.O.I. JR: What does being New Afrikan mean to you, and why did you choose this ideology?

SANYIKA: This answer flows right from the point i was just making about how to study and then having the corresponding material available to make coherent sense of what one has and is experiencing. See, one thing about colonialism as a method of control and exploitation, it is dynamic and flexible. That is, it is capable of morphing, melding and adapting to most any circumstance. It has to, in order to continue to exist. This has baffled us for years and has allowed our enemies to escape time and time again, as We stumbled blindly around trying to make sense of it. And no sooner do We learn its current shape and form, does it shape shift again and continue on.

Well, when i got to San Quentin in January of '86, on the tier was study material from the Black Liberation Movement (BLM), a lot of material from the Black Panther Party, the African People's Party, the African People's Socialist Party, etc. And as i said, i read it all.

But you see, that material had been written at a particular time to deal with a particular set of circumstances, you dig? The BLM had just caught up to how the enemy had morphed his set of methods on our control from old colonialism—slavery, Jim Crow—to neo-colonialism—civil rights, integration. And of course, this neo-colonialism was being rejected for Black Power—self-determination—by the youthful revolutionaries of that time. These youth were those who brought into existence the organizations i mentioned above.

They identified more with Malcolm and Black Power than with Martin and Negro Civil Rights. Cats were pushing a Nationalist line, recognizing, if only rudimentarily, that We were more of a nation inside of this empire than a disenfranchised "minority" of citizens of the empire. One can't be disenfranchised, if you've never been enfranchised, feel me?

So the empire, the capitalist-imperialist, was yet again morphing to live by implementing a neo-colonial system of Civil Rights and integration, and the Black Liberation Movement rejected that. And the material it printed to agitate, educate and organize clearly reflected this rejection of colonialism and neo-colonialism. Well, that's what i was turned on to when i hit the tier. However this was '86, and by then the BLM as a whole had been defeated.

Black Power had been turned into Black capitalism; so-called Black nationalism had been twisted into Black community control and other watered down appendages. And yet here We were reading and studying the same material used to combat a particular stage in our continual struggle and trying to apply it in a time that was not appropriate to its science. In other words, We overstood that We were still oppressed—but We were attempting to use outdated tools that no longer corresponded to the circumstances to get free.

We found ourselves stumbling blindly around the issues. We'd not taken into account the dynamism of our enemy's ability to morph. So i'm reading all the material, but i wasn't getting well. It wasn't cleansing me. It wasn't washing my eyes, my mind of colonialism. i could quote George, Robert Williams, Huey and Malcolm, but i couldn't make coherent sense of '86 amerika. So i became frustrated and i began to study for new tools to fight with.

This led me to the Black Liberation Army Coordinating Committee (BLA-CC). i got in touch with Sundiata Acoli, who in turn sent me to Owusu Yaki Yakubu, who was using the pseudonym Atiba Shanna at that time, and he began to send me the New Afrikan ideological material and things just cleaned up. What the comrades in the BLA-CC had done was go back and re-formulate, rebuild and reboot all the theories of the failed BLM and tie them together in a current ideo-theoretical line that corresponded perfectly to what was happening and what happened and what We should do for the future.

And they did this in *Notes from a New Afrikan POW Journal* (Books 1–7), *False Nationalism, False Internationalism* by E. Tani and Kai Sera, *Vita Wa Watu: a New Afrikan Theoretical Journal* (Books 8–12), *Settlers: Mythology of the White Proletariat* by J. Sakai. And finally through *Crossroad: A New Afrikan Captured Combatant Newsletter.*

So once the 'rads in the Army sent me this material, i could for the first time really feel the reality of our situation. And these were cats who had been on the frontlines of the BLM—in its armed formations—cats who were righteous revolutionaries. And too, i began to look at all the others who'd accepted the New Afrikan ideology—practically all of the POWs: Kuwasi Balagoon, Jalil Muntaqim, Sekou Odinga, Abdul Shanna, Sundiata Acoli, etc. So that was it for me. i dug into the ideological formation, overstood it and pressed on, in concert with those who'd proved themselves worthy in countless battles with the beast.

To be New Afrikan is to recognize that you are a member of a distinct culture, that you are a citizen of a nation unto itself in the belly of the beast. It is a determination to exert this national

reality, build a strong State (government) around it and struggle against the forces which oppress it in order to get free. And free here means free to determine our own destiny, free to develop our own productive forces to meet our needs as a nation, free to be ourselves for our own benefit and of course free of mind-warping genocidal violence perpetrated against our nationals from the cradle to the grave. This entails being free from capitalism, imperialism and colonialism.

To be a New Afrikan is to be guided by the New Afrikan Declaration of Independence [see pages 204–206], the New Afrikan Creed [see pages 202–203], and the Code of Umoja and the Nguzo Saba. It is to have allegiance to the Provisional Government of the Republic of New Afrika and to struggle to establish our sovereignty beyond contradiction. It's revolutionary nationalism.

M.O.I. JR: How successful was the [2011] Pelican Bay hunger strike?*

SANYIKA: Well, it was very successful in that it swung the spotlight this way and illuminated the draconian reality of our situation. In that sense it was very successful, more so than We had anticipated it would be. Of course, 12 years before the u.s. government opened Guantanamo Bay for so-called enemy combatants, California opened Pelican Bay for "threats to institutional security." No charges, no rules violations, no crimes—all politics. We've been shouting from under here since 1989.

We had a small hunger strike in 2001, but it wasn't well coordinated; however, it caught some attention. This one, however, has brought greater attention and some indignation. Our

_____

* See Appendix I for the Five Core Demands of this hunger strike.

demands are not irrational. We are only wishing, rather demanding, to be treated as human beings. We want those rights accorded to humans, but the system of imperialism cannot allow this. It cannot relent, because then who'd be the "boogey-man"?

How would they then justify all of this concrete and steel erected in this sleepy little logger town? We know that they are not going to put the citizens in here, not to any real degree anyway. these kamps are for nationals of internal colonies: New Afrika, Aztlán, Puerto Rico, Hawaii, Indigenous Nations, and those very few outlaws and anti-imperialists from their own empire.

That notwithstanding, We feel that the hunger strike brought some needed attention to this kamp. Of course We are trying to set up the groundwork for a new Prison Movement, since so many of us are here.

M.O.I. JR: Can you talk about your daily routine in Pelican Bay?

SANYIKA: The thing about being a prisoner—whether in a solitary situation like this or a mainline situation—is you either do the time or the time will do you. And what i mean by that is if a day goes by and you haven't learned nothing—a new word, a new location on the map, made a new breakthrough in old thinking or thought of and put into practice new ways of realizing it—then by and large you have wasted a day. If you sit around and get hypnotized by the TV, sports or gossip about who's gonna get kicked off of "Big Brother" or, as Gil Scott Heron said, "If Dick finally got down with Jane on Search For Tomorrow," then time is doing you. That's my motto.

So what i do is mind, body and spirit work all day. Study and struggle. i'm only allowed 10 books at a time. So i make them 10 count. Right now i'm working with *Meditiations on Frantz Fanon's Wretched of the Earth*, by Yaki Yakubu, *Pacifism as*

Pathology by Ward Churchill, *Block Reportin'* by you, *Our Enemies in Blue* by Kristian Williams, *Re-Thinking New Orleans* by Butch Lee and J. Sakai, *Lockdown America* by Christian Parenti, *We Are Our Own Liberators* by Jalil Muntaqim, *Settlers* by J. Sakai, and a host of periodicals and loose papers.

So with me it's ideological, theoretical and philosophical studies. As a theoretician, my thing is the mechanics of struggle. We are looking for ways of struggle that correspond to our particular set of circumstances. We are now in a post neo-colonial era. With this sock puppet Obama up there, it's a new day of the system morphing. We gotta keep up. It's no longer "Uncle Tom preachers"; it's Uncle Tom Supreme Kourt justices and Uncle Tom presidents, you dig?

So this cage is my classroom, my gym, my struggle chamber. i gotta be ready for my next and upcoming encounter with the beast. Study, write, exercise, think. That's my routine, all day every day. i gotta be better than i was before, better than our enemies. i'm very intent on making this time in this terrible place work for us and our national liberation struggle. And i can't help but want to make our enemies sorry for ever having treated any of us this way. i'm driven by both love and hate. It's dialectical.

M.O.I. JR: Can you tell us a little bit about the case you are locked up on now?

SANYIKA: In 2006, i was put on the FBI's Most Wanted list, the LAPD's Top Ten Most Wanted List, and became a fugitive with a $50,000 bounty on my head. Of course, i was never "on the run." Never ran. In fact, a few times i went looking for them.

A guy who was supposed to be about something was physically disciplined for transgressions in the area, and he defected to the amerikan Security Forces instead of correcting his behavior.

This was an opportunity they'd been waiting for, and so they said i beat this guy up and took his car. And here's the thing: Well, once i'd been captured by a joint effort of u.s. marshals, FBI and LAPD, this guy recanted his story and said he'd lied, and this and that. But by then the die had been cast. They spent $50,000 on paying an informant to tip them off, and i spent $50,000 on attorney fees to avoid a life term.

They brought in special attorneys for the prosecution and came with all kinds of propaganda and what have you. And We deflected all of that. i ended up with six years with 85 percent for carjacking, even though the guy recanted and two others were actually caught in the car and no one could corroborate his story. i was sent straight back here to the Bay. i've been validated with an indeterminate SHU term since 1989. As it stands, i am due out in 2012.

M.O.I. JR: What do you think about the State killing Tookie and the reason they gave?

SANYIKA: i had the very fortunate lot of knowing Tookie personally. We lived on the same street in South Central. His old hood became my hood when my set started. i loved him. The State, We have to keep in mind, is a representative of the government. The u.s. government is the tool used by the ruling class to administer its business, America Inc.

Overstanding it this way, We can see clearly that Tookie, like Tupac, like Eazy E, like George Jackson, like Malcolm and Martin and countless others, was "bad for business." These killings, public and obvious as they are, serve as psychological demonstrations to keep the masses traumatized against struggle. These killings are used as shocks and strains on the mass psychology of the people, and that's on the national level.

On the local level, there's other means and ways, as with Oscar Grant, Devin Brown, Tyisha Miller, etc. These they don't necessarily think will be national; they serve as local shocks and strains. It's a genocidal tactic utilized by law enforcement to keep the natives in line. Street organizations are allowed to function in certain areas, based on the same principle and strategy. Lateral warfare has always served the system. With Tookie, it was a national message, and it's a testament to the weakness of our forces that We allow such blatant acts of murder to happen to our nationals.

They, according to their own pathology, had to murder Tookie. He'd transformed himself into a formidable opponent of oppression, this on top of already being a stalwart street combatant and a leader. The beast couldn't afford to let him live. What i can say though is that he died well—head up, chest out, glaring menacingly at the enemies—no crying or wringing of the hands in sorrowful gestures. No, it's like Che said, "Go on, cowards. You'll only be killing a man."

M.O.I. JR: What role does the Prison Movement play in the overall people's movement in your analysis?

SANYIKA: It's the same as George said, the same as Sundiata Acoli posited, and the same as Owusu Yaki Yakubu pointed out: The Prison Movement must serve as a relevant part of the overall National Independence Movement by utilizing its capacity to teach, research, develop and produce able minded cadres for struggle. Some comrades have life or lengthy prison sentences and may not get out unless We liberate them, so their thing is prison reform work for better living conditions inside the kamps—though this is secondary to study and struggle around the picking, developing, maintenance and moving of cadres in concert with the overall National Liberation Struggle.

Prisoners and the Prison Movement will play just as important a role as students, workers and the military. It is just one more place We find ourselves that needs agitating, education and organization. In order to rebuild our organizations and our movement, We'll need competent cadres—professional revolutionaries—that can handle the tasks at hand. Cadres will come from all sectors of our nation and all classes. Prisoners will invariably fall into this, simply because it is the nature of the beast to capture and imprison us to the degree it does. Again, it's dialectical.

M.O.I. JR: What should be done to bring street and prison organizations closer together to support one another?

SANYIKA: When i first was captured, as i said, there were still remnants of the old Black Liberation Movement around—largely publications, periodicals, books etc. as well as these invited letters, communications and exchanges of ideas from inside and out.

But you see, the old Prison Movement was a reflection of the movement at large. That is, those who'd been captured came from organizations and formations on the street: the Black Panther Party, the Black Liberation Army, the African People's Party, the Nation of Islam, etc. They in turn contributed to the development of the Prison Movement. When the Black Liberation Movement, however, was defeated, collapsing first from its own weaknesses and then from the weight of the State's blows—COINTELPRO, counterinsurgency, etc.—the Prison Movement, too, collapsed.

With the death of Comrade George and then the Attica Massacres, the death knell was sounded across the empire. The thing is We are re-building now, but it's going to take communication, patience and honest, genuine struggle around issues of grave importance. The most fundamental things are ideology, theory and philosophy. These are weaknesses that allowed for our enemies to get in on us last time.

See, it's like this: Who are We—New Afrikans, Blacks, African-Americans? This is ideology. How do We get free—liberate our own nation from the u.s., integrate into a multicultural empire of amerika or go back to Afrika? This is theory. What tools do We use to get free? Do We rely on the metaphysical, believing that some god is going to help us, do We use the theories given to us by our enemies or do We use dialectical materialism? This is philosophy. We have to struggle around these in order to rebuild our organizations and movement, so We'll be on one accord.

M.O.I. JR: Lil' Bunchy (Dhanifu) is facing Three Strikes. Do you think that the government targets conscious street leaders and why?

SANYIKA: Again, like Tookie, i have the pleasure to know Dhanifu personally—a beautiful Brother and a fierce opponent to oppression. The oppressor has the luxury of having a long memory, of being able to strategize far into the future, to project, you dig? And unlike us, who have to contend with day to day struggles, the beast is on some future-of-the-empire stuff.

So when opportunities present themselves, such as with Dhanifu and this weapons charge, the enemy will swoop in and take full advantage of any given situation. It is the essence of their power over us. We cannot afford to sleep, slip or stumble. We have to be on all of the time. The beast is on all of the time. Ain't no off switch on national oppression ever.

That is, until the people turn it off. We have to believe our own spiel, that the beast is merciless and will go to any length to eradicate our resistance so it won't develop into a revolution. The beast is trying to protect its way of life. If that means murkin', capturing and torturing all of us, then that is what it will do. In closing, anyone who has the vaguest notions about the length the amerikan ruling class will go to maintain dominance or to answer your question about targeting conscious leaders should read *The FBI War on Tupac Shakur and Black Leaders* by John Potash. That's the answer and the ample proof. In closing, i'd like to say We appreciated all the support for our hunger strike and all the work you and Comrade Fred Hampton Jr. do. Rebuild!

Study and Struggle:
An Overstanding

> _Who Are We_, those of us who would build a national "black"
> prisoners organization? There is much hard evidence to
> show that as each day passes, more and more "black" pris-
> oners identify themselves as _New Afrikans_ and work on
> behalf of _the New Afrikan Independence Movement_.
> Atiba Shanna[*]

Across the expanse of a couple of decades, We've seen the political
consciousness of prisoners grow in proportion with their overstanding of what it actually means to be a prisoner in amerikkka,
but also as nationals of captive nations held in partial paralysis
by u.s. imperialism. Prisoners have slowly begun to take an objective view of the matrix of u.s. colonialism from a dialectical
perspective that informs us that the settler government holds,
dominates and exploits both external/internal colonies. And that
the old facade of "disadvantaged minorities" is giving way to the
stark reality of submerged nations here under the blurry veneer
of a so-called "united states."

This developing consciousness springs from a Revolutionary Nationalist overstanding of social development. Informed by

---

[*] Atiba Shanna, _Notes from a New Afrikan P.O.W. Journal,_ Book Three
(emphasis in original).

even the most rudimentary application of dialectical materialism, one is easily drawn to the reality of New Afrika, Aztlán, Puerto Rico, Hawaii, Alaska and the Indigenous peoples being submerged and colonized—whole nations existing under the false patina of amerikkkanism.

The greater our overstanding of this reality, the less We are believing in, or relying on, the old obviously false social construct of "race" to define ourselves and other oppressed people. Color, or "race," as a binary term to describe the shallow differences between humans—having no scientific basis in reality—is not a deep enough, not sound or reasonable enough, overstanding to explain, confront and resolve our problems.

It's been said that "the color of freedom in amerikkka is green." This tells us something about the false construct of "race," no? It hints at the *fact* that under the rubble of "race" is bedrock. And that bedrock, that solid foundation, is economics. Is capitalism. We can't even discuss, or We shouldn't even discuss, "racism" without mentioning and combining it with capitalism. For capitalism built the social construct of "race" around itself as a motto, a defense and a justification for prolonged activity. Capitalism is the *material* manifestation; "race" is the *shadow*, or immaterial reality of what casts it—as a consequence of the original form. It's not that it's wholly unreal. We can *see* it. The shadow, i mean. We can even feel it. But it is but a reflection: We'll exhaust ourselves to the point of madness trying to combat it alone without applying destructive force to the material thing that it reflects. To be "anti-racist" is to be anti-capitalist. We become anti-racists by not using binary terms constructed to promote and sustain "race."

Any attempt to destroy "racism" without an explicit link to the struggle against capitalism ultimately serves only to reinforce "racist" ideology and to shield capitalism from

attack. On the other hand, an attempt to combat capital-
ism without an explicit link to anti-racist discourse and
struggle allows capitalism to use the belief in "race" held
by oppressed peoples and appeal to the "racism" of citizens
of the oppressive state, thus undermining all revolutionary
initiative.

This combat also requires that We begin to de-link our-
selves from the use of language that reinforces and repro-
duces racial ideology, e.g. the terms "white" and "black" in
reference to the identity of peoples. *

In our developing consciousness, which is necessarily New
Afrikan, revolutionary and nationalist, We are needing new tools,
new language, new ideas, means and ways to re-build ourselves
into a coherent whole for movement and struggle. We are talking about cadre development. This will come about only through
arduous study and struggle.

See, here's the basic thing: if you are calling yourself a New
Afrikan, then you are at once saying that you are *not* an amerikkkan (of any stripe). You are rejecting the reactionary/colonial
identity placed arbitrarily on you by the enemy culture. You are
implying that you are a citizen of the Republic of New Afrika.
Further, this means that you overstand that a *New* Afrikan nation exists and has existed, in north amerikkka, at least since
1660. Now, "nation" here is not to be confused with a *State* or *government*. A nation is a cultural/custom/linguistic social development that is consolidated and evolves on a particular land mass
and shares a definite collective awareness of itself.

---

* James Yaki Sayles [Atiba Shanna], *Meditations on Frantz Fanon's
Wretched of the Earth: New Afrikan Revolutionary Writings*. (Montreal:
Kersplebedeb 2010), pp. 157–8.

New Afrika, as a distinct entity, a totally working-class *nation*, has existed since 1660 here. The nation was given shape, name, general laws and a creed in 1968, with the founding of the Provisional Government by over five hundred New Afrikan nationalists. Established at this historic convention was, the New Afrikan Declaration of Independence, Code of Umoja (New Afrikan Constitution) and the New Afrikan Creed. A President, Vice-Presidents, People's Center Councils and a People's Revolutionary Leadership Council were elected to designate New Afrikan Population Districts, set up registration for a New Afrikan census, etc. This was the forming of a *State*, an organized body designed to coherently give shape and form to the already long existing New Afrikan nation.

So, We are not trying to "create" a nation—the nation exists. We are trying to agitate, educate and organize the nation for Land, Independence and Socialism. This can only be realized

Members of the Republic of New Afrika hold a press conference. Present are Robert Williams, Sr., Mabel Robinson Williams, Queen Mother Moore, Gaidi Abiodun Obadele and Imari Abubakari Obadele.

through revolution. And despite what We've recently seen in North Africa with their "Arab Spring," We are under no illusions about our struggle here being a protracted, long drawn out, revolutionary war. And, truthfully, necessarily so. We have a lot of cleansing to do after existing so close to the seat of world power for so long. We overstand our level of contamination.

We are talking about being ideologically consistent. About pushing a particular line. Again, i want to go to Comrad Yaki because his instructions are profound:

> *Angolan, Russian, Algerian, Chinese, French, Vietnamese, Cuban, Korean, Tanzanian—these are nationalities. Our nationality is New Afrikan. We don't refer to ourselves as "black" because We don't base our nationality (nor our politics) on "race" or color or a biological element of our being. Social factors are the primary determinations of our national identity (and our politics).*

The same reason We don't call ourselves "black" is also why We don't call ourselves "African-American," or "negro," "colored," etc. These are *chains*, which tie us to the plantation, to the colonial system. These are terms that substantiate, promote and sustain the colonial mentality and thus our oppression. Again, Comrad Yaki's words instruct:

> *The "Native," the "Negro," the "colored," the "black" and the "African-American" have no identity apart from that given them by the colonizer—that is, not unless they <u>resist</u> colonialism, which entails: 1) their maintenance of an identity that is separate and distinct from that of the colonizer; 2) they begin to develop a <u>new</u> identity, through*

---

* Ibid., p. 154.

*the process of "decolonization"—through having remained
separate and distinct, colonized people aren't who they
were prior to colonization and they can't return to the
past. Colonization has arrested their independent development, distorted who they are, and now they must become
a <u>new</u> people during the process by which they regain their
independence.*[*]

Let's go a bit into this. Those who are calling themselves "African-
Americans" are really doing so for two reasons. First, of course,
there is an implicit overstanding that runs thoroughly through
the New Afrikan nation that We are not *really* amerikkkans. That
We are in fact a people/nation unto ourselves. This used to be
widely overstood with little notion of anything to the contrary.
Neo-colonialism has worked obsessively to change this awareness.
The rapid de-colonization ("de-segregation") of the nation, beginning in the late 1950s, ushered in a new (neo) more thorough,
and dare i say, *revolutionary*, form of control and exploitation:
neo-colonialism. "Blacks" took over from "negroes" to lead the
masses into an integrated lockstep with capitalism, while they
(the misleaders) were awarded nominal posts in local and regional
government. Because the bourgeois media postulated these class
enemies as being "successful," in a new and improved amerikkka,
it fostered an image (crafted by Madison Avenue) that anybody
could make it. "Now that segregation is over, you can grow up to
be anything you want." Except free, of course.

The more integration (which was supposed to mean "freedom and equality") We got, the worse our predicament became.
The more bourgeois "freedom and equality" We struggled to obtain, the more critical our existence became, the stronger the

---

[*] Ibid., p. 168.

"black" bourgeoisie got—compounded a hundred times by the u.s. ruling class. The stronger the "black" bourgeoisie became, the more our revolutionary leadership was attacked, assassinated, imprisoned, or exiled. The more this became so, the worse the hoods got. The worse the hoods got, the more street orgs began to proliferate. More dope, more guns, more pigs—more prisons. This is what the losing of a sense of self brings. Integration *is* neo-colonialism. And it's reactionary nationalism. But it would be unfair to say it's not *progress*. It *is* progress—it's just not progress in *our* interest. We are moving forward, but it is towards our annihilation.

The "black" bourgeoisie worked in tandem with its masters to keep the chains on New Afrika. They overstood the strong nationalist sentiment that ran through the nation. So in order to placate this sentiment and please their masters, the "black" bourgeoisie introduced the term "African-American." A split personality that straddled an ocean and a colonial existence. But because our "leaders" said it was right and, "After all," the masses said, "We are Africans"—Voila! This, of course, is not scientific or a reflection of any true reality. It is a term used to maintain a colonial relationship with New Afrika—now being run by remote control through the antics and colorful animation of the "African-American" bourgeoisie. You see them in the Congressional Black Caucus, the higher echelons of the Prince Hall Masons, in the persons of Oprah, Jesse, Al Sharpton, Robert Johnson, etc. They've been appointed by the u.s. ruling class to lead the masses—into a neo-colonial marriage with amerikkka. The "African American" bourgeoisie is conjoined (face to ass) with the u.s. ruling class and no surgery short of protracted people's war will loosen them and free us.

The masses, by and large, are innocently confused—they can be redeemed. It is our job as cadres to do that. Which is why it is so important to study and struggle—to build up your revolutionary ideological, philosophical and theoretical overstanding so as to be able to distinguish the real from the false. The righteous from the reactionary.

> *Our vision must be emphasized in opposition to the imperialist and neo-colonialist perspectives. Our vision demands that We stress the need to establish New Afrikan state power as the <u>prerequisite</u> for the long term resolution of colonial violence, bad housing, miseducation, poor health, no jobs, etc.*
>
> *At present, the orientation underlying mass struggle is primarily neo-colonialist. We ask the u.s. government to do things for us. Our struggle is <u>against</u> the u.s. government, to secure the power to prevent it from doing things to us and so that We can do things for ourselves, under our own government.*
>
> *Each issue that the masses struggle around must be infused (by the people's vanguard) with the idea that none of our problems can be solved until We achieve national independence...* [*]

In closing then, i'd like to simply emphasize the need to study and struggle. Study revolutionary nationalism and struggle around the issues that are affecting us. It's a beautiful thing to see more prisoners becoming conscious of themselves as New Afrikans; this too is a prerequisite to getting free. Change your mind and you can change your conditions. Overstanding and appreciating the reality of one's situation gives one a greater sense of

---

[*] Atiba Shanna, "On What It Means to 'Re-Build'," *Vita Wa Watu: A New Afrikan Theoretical Journal*, Book 12, April 1988, p. 34.

appreciation for other oppressed nationals in the same or similar predicaments.

i'm gonna fall out with a quote by Comrad Yaki that pretty much sums it all up—

> *Anyone claiming to attack racism while claiming that racism is the only thing wrong with this system, is either terribly confused or an outright enemy of the people and their interests. If We truly wanna get rid of racism, We have to overthrow capitalism... first.*[*]

---

[*] Sayles, p. 331.

Class Antagonisms Inside the Fundamental Contradiction of National Oppression

Having just passed the nineteenth, and quickly approaching the twentieth, anniversary of the L.A. Rebellion,* We should be reminded here of what Rodney King whimpered as he stood in front of a bank of microphones surrounded by class enemies and neo-colonial politicians.

We should remember how he'd been dressed in that non-threatening cardigan sweater, white shirt, and black tie. How his hair had been tortured into submission by a jheri curl. We should reflect, as well, upon how timid and spooked he looked and on how concerned and stern those who flanked him were as well. That was a Kodak moment. It was staged to foster an image of contrition and resignation. Submission. A *victim*.

Rodney King had been led to believe, thru a bourgeois sense of reasoning, that the Rebellion was really about *him*. That the reason New Afrikans and Mexicanos took to the streets of South Central was the result of his filmed beating.

---

* The L.A. Rebellion, April 29 to May 1, 1992. This is the "official" time-line. However, it took the security forces (police—above and under-cover—CHP, sheriffs and national guard) at least seven days to regain full control of rebel areas.

That, of course, is typical of mechanical, bourgeois think-ing. What it's not typical of, however, is someone from the hood.[*] And this cuts both ways. No one in the hoods and barrios *ever* thought it was about Rodney King. We'd all seen the film, over and over like everyone else. But that was par for the course. We'd *always* seen that—long before anyone had caught it on tape.

Actually, We'd experienced much more than that. Why it's safe to say that hoods have gone to *war* with each other, in vicious waves of internal (intra-class) combat, for much *less* than that. Though, because of a general colonial mentality, which prevents the challenging of (from bottom up) oppression, the same "hood" forces will *not*, in any systematic way, wage war on the pigs! Or *for* Freedom, Land and Socialism.[†]

Rodney King alone and of his own accord would *not* have thought to hold a press conference to ask the asinine question (in the form of a whimpered request), *"Can't we all just get along?"* The fact of the matter was that *We* were getting along. New Afrikans and Mexicanos *were* getting along just fine. What We *couldn't*

---

[*] Suffice it to say that those of us in the hoods and barrios have always had a running battle with the LAPD and L.A. Sheriff's Department. We've never found it expedient to hold press conferences to highlight either our beatings nor our attacks on them. We took our lumps, just as We gave them theirs.

[†] What prevents hood forces from systematic—i.e. organized and sustained—combat, is the colonial mentality. This mentality sees the State and its operators as legitimate and reflects upon itself as not. Thus, ultimately the lumpen submits to the "legitimate authority" and allows the State to carry out its function—which is to dominate, oppress and exploit. For further reading on the criminal/colonial men-tality see: *Notes From A New Afrikan P.O.W. Journal, Book One* (Spear & Shield Publications) and James Yaki Sayles, *Meditations On Frantz Fanon's Wretched of the Earth*, especially pages 63–86.

overstand was why he was admonishing *us* for getting at the exploiters of our communities? The impression he gave, with his handlers' hands up his back like a ventriloquist doll, was that a "race riot"[*] was going on. As if We had begun to kill *each other*, or burn and rob *each other's* homes. His handlers compelled him to send up a false flag—a diversion. But, you see, this was the very thing that exposed the class interests and reactionary politics of the Uncle Toms that had been designated to handle him and by extension us![†]

---

[*] i put both *race* and *riot* in quotations because, of course, both are misnomers—false flags designed to not just mis-inform, but to *distort* the reality. There are no "races." There's but the human race. Nor was the Rebellion a "riot": that term was deliberately used to de-legitimize, to belittle and confuse. And of course no reports of private homes or national clashes were reported—or seen.

[†] For a critical breakdown and overstanding of the black petty bourgeoisie, see: J. Sakai, *Settlers: Mythology of the White Proletariat* (Morningstar Press, 1989).

Let's go back for a minute, let's talk social development ("history"). There exists a fundamental contradiction in our lives that, like an elephant in the room, no one wants to acknowledge. As a consequence of the war waged upon various Afrikan nations by European powers, those of us captured and kidnapped were taken out of our own self-determining social developments and violently forced into euro-amerikan *his*-tory. This is not simply a clever play on words. This is a reality. We lost the ability to control *our own destiny.*[*] Read that again.

From that time until now, the fundamental (basic) contradiction between the u.s. oppressor nation and our own oppressed and colonized nation, has been the governing imperialist relationship. Which is to say, *us* not being in control of the *qualitative factors*[†] that determine our lives as a people. A Nation!

Our tradition of struggle against this fundamental contradiction has taken many forms—some hidden or obscured, and some open and hostile. But all of these have been to resolve the

---

[*] A people's sovereignty is measured by its ability to control, chart and determine its own destiny. That is, who it trades with, who it is, who it gets along with and who it doesn't. For example, the Provisional Government of the Republic of New Afrika is not at war with Afghanistan—*but*, the u.s. has so blurred the reality of our national reality, that not only do Afghani people believe that all the people in the political borders of amerika are at war with them, the actual colonial subjects of captive nations believe it as well. Thus, even though the PG-RNA is not at war with the Afghanis, it has literally no control over its nationals to prevent them from going to war on behalf of the u.s. oppressor nation. It does not have the power to control our national destiny.

† Of course, the qualitative factors are education, health care, employment, judiciary and housing. All these are administered at a hefty and often mind-warping and spirit-breaking cost by the colonialists!

fundamental contradiction and to regain our independence.[*]
While there have been bona fide struggles to resolve the contradiction, there have also been reactionary neo-colonial struggles,
waged by internal enemies loyal to the oppressor nation and culture, that have tried time and time again to subvert and control
our destiny for the benefit of the capitalists.[†]

They've come among us, always imposed from above, stir-
ring up emotions and giving lip service to "progress," "equality,"
"justice" and "prosperity." These always *within* the colonial confines of the oppressors' arrangements.[‡] And none, collectively,
ever materialize, because without a resolution of the fundamental
contradiction—that is, the freeing of our productive forces from

---

[*] As revolutionary nationalists We reject the notion and line that says
our freedom is to be found or "won" by integrating into and becoming
"equal" with the very system responsible for our oppression and the
people who administer that domination. Therefore We look to the lines
of struggle which have sought to regain independence from—out and
away of—the colonialists, e.g. the Garvey Movement, Henry Highland
Garnet, Pap Singleton, the BLM and NAIM, and similar national liberation struggles here and abroad—all anti-imperialist struggles.

[†] See: J. Sakai, *Settlers: Mythology of the White Proletariat*, Chapter 4:
Neo-Colonialism & Leadership.

[‡] Here you have to visualize Al Sharpton, Rev. Jesse Jackson, MLK Jr.,
etc. These are our "leaders" not because We have chosen them—or
because they speak our aspirations to power, but because our enemies
have chosen them to mis-interpret our aspirations to fit into the
colonial scheme of national oppression. Hence at *every* outbreak of
struggle, whether it's the L.A. Rebellion or the Jena 6 issue, Mumia's
case or the Occupy the Hood struggle in Oakland—here come the neo-
colonialists not to help us, but to do reconnaissance for the enemy. To
find out what's going on and then to report it, get instructions on how
to twist it, then jump opportunistically out in front to mis-lead it right
back into the clutches of the colonial parameters. That's the function of
this class.

u.s. imperialism and the governing of our own affairs—We'll remain a "minority" *within* the amerikan system (as opposed to a *majority* in our own) and subjected to the established bourgeois social contract, i.e. *colonialism*. Neo & Post.*

We can parade all thru the empire with "black" congressmen, "black" mayors, "black" governors, "black" police chiefs, "black" supreme kourt justices—hell, even a "black" president—and *absolutely nothing* will alter the genocidal relationship that governs our national oppression here because the "blacks" are a part of the colonial apparatus. They have made a strategic alliance with the capitalist-imperialists to act as go-betweens in our oppression and exploitation.†

---

* We should clarify this term "post-colonialism." Ward Churchill pretty much summed this up when he said: "...how about we actually complete the process of global decolonization *before* we announce our entry into 'the postcolonial era'?" (Ward Churchill, *On the Justice of Roosting Chickens*. [AK Press, 2003]) Truly, how can We be in a *post* (after) colonial era when colonialism *still* exists??

† In our struggle—inside the colonial reality of New Afrika and its struggle to identify itself in the sea of imperialist distortion and neo-colonial *ignoration*—which, as Ward Churchill points out, is deeper than mere ignorance. Ignoration is: "...instead to be informed and then to *ignore* the information." So, to be ignorant is *not* to know, but *ignoration* is to know, but to ignore. Churchill says: "there is a vast difference between not knowing and not caring...." (Churchill, p. 7.) So, here We are trying to show that *within* the New Afrikan nation there is a class struggle between those who identify themselves as "black" or "African American" and New Afrikans. And further, that those petty bourgeois forces are actually *conscious* of themselves as go-betweens in order to steer the masses wrong (rightward) and serve *their* class interests and that they deftly employ ignoration. So, when We use "black" here it is to direct attention to this class and their role as collaborators. Like the "negroes" Malcolm called out when first bringing "black" into existence.

This is a conscious class stand. The "black" petty bourgeoisie is not innocently confused, like say Mrs. Johnson across the street is, about our national oppression. About the existence and subjugation of New Afrika. They are well-read, have travelled and are experienced—they have just chosen sides against us and in favor of our historical enemies! And, the sooner We recognize and internalize this, the better off We'll be.[*]

Black ain't nothing but a color. As a designation of our national identity it has played out. It is a superficial overstanding at best and a *foolish* and *dangerous* analysis at worst.[†]

We have no collective control over the qualitative factors which determine our lives. We do not, in other words, control our destiny. Not as a people (nation) or a State (government). We are not a free, self-determining people. We were, before contact, kidnapping and national oppression—but not now. Until this fundamental contradiction is resolved, until New Afrika is independent of u.s. imperialism and neo-colonial domination, We will remain at the continual mercy of our historical enemies and

---

[*] *Ignoration.*

[†] To label oneself "black" or others "white," "brown" or "red," is to fall into the ideological trap of racism. It is to believe and propagate the false social construct that humans are broken down into different "races" which are classified outwardly by the complexion of one's skin, or the texture of one's hair. Though, of course, it's deeper than this since it also promulgates one's superiority and inferiority according to those who designed it. What it essentially does is bury the reality of class and politics—the real social determinants of humans. Humans are all *one* race. No matter if you subscribe to racism or not, if you're using terms like black, white or brown to determine yourself or others *you* are pushing a racist line. See: Sayles (Kersplebedeb, 2010). We'll use these terms in quotations to point to their un-reality. Or in distinguishing New Afrikan revolutionary nationalists from petty bourgeois collaborators.

their warped worldview. A worldview that breeds, promotes, encourages and finances predation and exploitation!

Which brings us back to Rodney King and "Can't We All Just Get Along." The question that begs an answer is: *Who* is this "We" he spoke of? The rebellion was *against* what was generally perceived as the system and particularly *against* exploiters who parasitically attached themselves to our oppression, chose to bleed our communities of the little finances We were able to have. The masses, in their choice of targets, were only reappropriating the wealth they'd invested in these stores and businesses that were then taking that wealth out of the hoods and barrios and giving it to the enemies of us all. So *"We,"* the poor and exploited, were already "getting along" with each other. Who We *didn't* get along with were those who'd exploited us. Who'd bled our areas dry of finances while flooding our areas with a bunch of crap and b.s.

It wasn't the Crips, Bloods or Surenos[*] who'd pulled Rodney King out of his car and beat the hell out of him. Nor was it the Black Liberation Army or the Brown Berets. So, why was his press conference directed at *us* in the hoods and barrios? This

---

[*] Here We use the three dominant street orgs in L.A.—Crips, Bloods and Surenos (Southsiders)—to point up the reality that those on the front lines in the initial stages of the Rebellion were, in fact, street org combatants who'd felt a sense of pride and control over their areas. Of course, the grassroots—the students, working class and the elderly— eventually came out en masse and kept it going. And, here, the Surenos (Southsiders) are the conglomerate "Latino" street orgs that function under the 13 (or Trece) numerology.

also alerted us to who it was who had arranged this press conference. The next question in line with his request is: What exactly did he mean by "*get along*"? As in, "Can we all *get along*?"

Didn't our "getting along" with national oppression lead us to this point? Didn't We "*just get along*" after they *kidnapped* us, *colonized* us, *hung* us, *neo-colonized* us, *imprisoned* us, *ghetto-ized* us, *miseducated* us, *un-employed* us, *assassinated* our leaders, *drugged* us, *infected* us* and sent our youth to *fight* other oppressed peoples for them? Didn't We get along during *all that*? Getting "along" with u.s. imperialism and our own genocide, has gotten us into this sordid ass state.

"Getting along" allowed the pigs to feel comfortable with pulling Rodney King out of his car and beating the hell out of him. The pigs didn't fear reprisal from the Black Liberation Army for harming one of our nationals because when they imprisoned our combatants We "just got along" with that. *Re-read that.*†

But you see, here's the thing—those were not Rodney King's words, nor his thoughts. Probably not even his will. No, those who were pulling his vocal cords were those who had a vested interest, a stake, in the system—as it was *before* the Rebellion. Those who had made a political and economic (class) alliance—with the imperialists! His now famous quote was actually a

---

* "Infected us" points to the various government tactics of smallpox (Trail of Tears), syphilis (Tuskeegee study, 1932 to 1972), HIV, hypertension, hepatitis, etc.

† To recognize political prisoners of war is to recognize the reality of the Nation. We feel that the low level of national consciousness—so few are aware that they are colonial subjects of captive nations—directly correlates with the low levels of recognition and support for our captured combatants. Some of the longest held prisoners of war hail from internal colonies (New Afrika, Puerto Rico, Aztlán and the Indigenous Nations) here inside the u.s. of a.

message from our class enemies by way of someone who they *thought* We could identify with. But, of course, his (their) words fell upon deaf ears because those who'd been treated just as bad (and some even worse) were out in the streets looking for a better day.

All the things people labored so hard to manufacture, at minimum wage jobs, but could not afford to buy, they got for *free*. People were getting food, clothing, diapers, shoes and whatever else they could never afford, but always needed. And this in an empire whose wealth began upon their conquests and continues upon their exploitation today. Let us not forget that the u.s., as an empire, has never supported itself—*ever!* It was born a parasite and grew to prominence—as a parasite. It is today a parasite. But in the wealthiest empire on the planet, in the history of the world, people are *starving, homeless* and generally *without*.

The repression required to keep us "just getting along" is a massive effort undertaken by every branch of the oppressor government: Executive, Legislative and Judiciary. In fact, laws are enacted to maintain bourgeois hegemony over both internal and external colonies. Both Federal (national) and State (regional) laws function to keep the oppressed tethered to the *floor* of the empire.* There is a general and permanent state of war that governs all relations between oppressor and oppressed. Sometimes it's hidden and tactically called something else—usually something with a benign name that sounds well-meaning. You know, like "War on Poverty" or "War on Drugs" or "War on Gangs." They militarize *everything* having to do with relations between oppressed and oppressor nations. It's all part and parcel of the general and permanent state of war between us and them! And just because We ain't ready, organized and responding to it *don't mean*

---

* See Michelle Alexander, *The New Jim Crow* (New Press, 2010).

it's not a war. The hoods, barrios and reservations are virtual prisons. The schools are halfway houses and the prison industrial complex is doing big business. It's a war alright. Ready or not.*

A permanent state of war *must* exist in order to maintain fear in and control over the internal colonies. This permanent state of war is called *colonialism*. When they allow someone who looks like you to govern you, for them—this is called neo (new) colonialism. And, when they let a "black" run the business, as in Rock Bottom being president of the u.s.—this is called post-neo-colonialism. But colonialism all the same. The system is capable of morphing at a moment's notice in order to survive and continue to oppress. As Butch Lee pointed out, "It can even appear as its opposite in order to evade destruction." The slogan popularized by the old Black Liberation Movement, "By Any Means Necessary," actually *embodies* what the u.s. system of capitalism is *really* about. In practice. *Always*.†

They will select a "black" sock puppet to be the president to demonstrate to their investors that they are color blind—and

* See John Potash, *The FBI War On Tupac Shakur & Black Leaders* (Progressive Left Press, 2007).
† See Ward Churchill, *Perversions of Justice: Indigenous Peoples and Anglo-American Law* (City Lights, 2003).

then turn right around and imprison 800,000 New Afrikans.[*] Then, the sock puppet president turns around and appoints various women to his team to show the people it is not patriarchal— but the same system is waging an authoritarian war on women and children. Though especially women and children of color— those from the internal colonies (New Afrika, Puerto Rico, Aztlán and Indigenous Nations).[†]

And, of course, We have to contend with the *loyal-enemies* of the empire. These are the ones who go hooping and hollering about "racism" and "discrimination"—boo-hooing about how *exclusionary* the system is—and yet they really only want *in*. They want "equality"—to be equal with the very ones they claim are "racists." They use terms like "*our* government," or "*our* troops in Afghanistan"—"*our* police force." They are clamoring against "discrimination" because they feel they, too, should be allowed to prey on people. They want to be "equal" *in* the system *of* capitalism. They don't want to *stop* the problem—they want to be a part of it. Why else would they ask for "equality" without calling into question the entire grotesque apparatus?[‡]

This is what makes the petty bourgeois class of "blacks" so dangerous. They have the resources, approval and backing of the

---

[*] Michelle Alexander, op cit.

[†] See: Butch Lee & Red Rover, *Night-Vision: Illuminating War and Class on the Neo-Colonial Terrain* (Vagabond Press, 1993).

[‡] There's another term We could use here to describe this class—or rather what this class suffers from: *cognitive dissonance*. This, on top of their *ignoration*. Cognitive dissonance, meaning: even when confronted with overwhelming evidence that what one perceives is wrong, one still, without fail, believes the contrary. It was coined by Dr. Leon Festinger, of the University of Chicago, in the 1950s. The petty bourgeoisie in order to sustain itself as a class of mis-leaders has to submit to a collective sense of cognitive dissonance and ignoration.

imperialists to carry on their campaigns of *accepted* forms of protest, *even when they appear to question* the bourgeois laws of the enemy. For instance: they'll support both a new trial and the release of Mumia Abu Jamal, *only because* We can prove that he was wrongly convicted as a part of a frame-up. And while *We* go on to link this frame-up with a total array of colonial maneuvers carried out to keep New Afrika oppressed and exploited, *they'll* pull back at "racism" and ignore our need for self-determination. This, because *their* class interests reach an end at calling into question the fundamental contradiction.* We can demonstrate this by the fact that there is no support for Sundiata Acoli, Jalil Muntaqim, Sekou Odinga or any other New Afrikan prisoners of war. Anything that points to the challenging of the fundamental contradiction—that calls into question the actual national oppression of New Afrika—the petty bourgeoisie will *ignore*, reject or outright deny support for. This would not be in accord with *their* class interests as parasites upon our misery, their collaboration with our oppressors. So, within the framework of their accepted forms of protests, as *loyal enemies* (as oppo-sames), they can call Mumia's capture, incarceration and conviction "racist," "discriminatory" and "questionable." But that's where it will end. Those are the parameters. That's the function of this class. To *appear* as staunch defenders of "black," or "African American," rights, progress and equality *only within* the boundaries of established imperial rule. Which is to say *only* as "citizens" of the oppressor nation—as "minorities" needing special handling. Victims.

---

* Even in giving lip service support to Mumia within the parameters of the bourgeois order, they did so only after the massive effort of the people grew too big to ignore. They safely laid in the cut and tailed safely behind.

And here We are back at Rodney King. Once the spontaneous L.A. Rebellion had run its course, brought under control only secondarily by the national guard—it's primary weakness, of course, was its spontaneity*—the u.s. government enacted a counterinsurgency policy called *Weed and Seed*. This directive was issued straight from the White House, from then-president George H.W. Bush. And, let us not forget, that this same pig had, from January 1976 to 1977 been Director of the Central Intelligence Agency. So he was no stranger to counterinsurgency programs.†

Weed and Seed was a counterinsurgency program much like the Phoenix Program run previously on the Vietnamese people

---

* We have to acknowledge what Comrade George Jackson coined the "Riot Stage" of social development and of consciousness. This stage is characterized by spontaneity and shortsightedness. Usually led by petty bourgeois sentiment and emotions. This, of course, is a weakness that is exploited by the enemy. They'd easily prefer a quick, spontaneous flare-up—a "riot"—to an entrenched, protracted people's war waged by the internal colonies. So, in portraying the Rebellion, even by calling it a "riot," they'll promote it as if it *really* was a great threat to the establishment. As revolutionaries, We have to point out that yes, We are glad to see that the masses have not been so lulled to sleep by the illusions of bourgeois democracy that they wouldn't resist at all. We simultaneously must stress that rebellions are not revolutions. That rebellions are, by and large, reformist. Since one can rebel *against* something without necessarily being *for* its opposite. Usually if it's spontaneous, this is the case. So while the L.A. Rebellion was *against* exploitation, pig repression and a general sense of oppression, it wasn't actually *for* Land, Independence and Socialism. Nor was it actually defined as anti-capitalist. But for us cadres it was a sign of collective life and a will to resist. Good soil to plant new seeds.

† For a very good breakdown on counterinsurgency, check out: Kristian Williams, *Our Enemies in Blue: Police and Power in America* (South End Press, 2007).

to, it explicitly said, "neutralize the Viet Cong by assassinating its cadres, destroying its bases among its people and strategically winning over the Vietnamese population." That is exactly what *Weed and Seed* was about as well. In the *hoods* and *barrios* of South Central.*

Once you see New Afrikans as an internal, colonized *nation* and not simply as a "black minority of discriminated against u.s. citizens," you'll begin to overstand the interchangeability of military tactics used against other colonies around the world. Not only did *Weed and Seed* implement a weeding out of "troublemakers"—i.e. combatants, leaders and political adversaries—but it *seeded* points of contention and distrust amongst the various participants in the Rebellion and Resistance that grew eventually into what's happening now between almost every hood and barrio. These conflicts did not fall from the sky. Their origins are on Earth, issuing from designs that serve someone's needs. The idea is to follow the conflicts to the point of interest. Which is to say, *who* is benefiting from the conflicts? Keep the term *Weed and Seed* in mind as We go forward here.

Nationals of two oppressed and colonized nations (Aztlán and New Afrika) are involved in shooting wars. Yes, these conflicts

---

* To show the audacity of the colonialists, since 1992 they have an actual program called the Weed & Seed Program which is at: 1133 Rhea Street, Long Beach, CA 90806. Website www.longbeach.gov/health/FSS/ws.asp. Here are the "services" it offers: "Clothing, mental health, counseling, social service information, low cost housing, drug and alcohol treatment, WIC, child care and schools. Also provides: education, career preparation, social and economic/life skills activities, job readiness skills, drug and gang prevention and education program and promotes educational programs to ex-offenders to assure work skills for employment." This is from its website. This is counterinsurgency disguised as a "helpful program."

largely involve lumpen (criminal) elements. Those involved in street org activity. The lumpen element to a degree played some significant roles in the revolution of the '60s and early '70s. Especially those who were able to transform their criminal mentalities into conscious revolutionary mentalities. Even though it's largely lumpen elements in contention in the hoods/barrios, regular, working-class people, students and children, are also being affected by these clashes. But the thing is, the combatants are nationals of *oppressed nations*—those the u.s. government has already deemed "social dynamite"* and has slated for liquidation thru one of its various methods of collective death and destruction. So, once the enemy culture saw the mass unity during the Rebellion, measures thru Weed and Seed were undertaken to *divide*, so as to be in a better position to <u>conquer</u>, these elements who obviously had no qualms about rebelling against oppression.

Here's one of the tactics they used: On Florence and Normandie Avenues, the acknowledged point of origin of the Rebellion, New Afrikans were shown on film pulling a Mexicano priest from his car, yanking his pants down while he was on the ground, and spray painting his private parts black. This was not what it actually was reported to be. While this priest was, in fact, Mexicano, he'd been pointed out by a Mexicano as a child molester and was thus disciplined by the first group that got to him. But because those who got him were New Afrikan and he was obviously a Mexicano and no sound was attached to the video, the media was allowed to mis-interpret the scene as they wished.

And this is what they did. So, there was Reginald Denny laid out after being pulled from his truck—after he'd yelled "get your black asses out of the street" to the rebels—and then beaten.

---

* See Christian Parenti, *Lockdown America: Police & Prisons in the Age of Crisis* (Verso, 1999).

And across the street was the Mexicano priest, pants pulled down, private parts painted black—and the rebels were seemingly targeting anyone who wasn't New Afrikan as they passed. This is what it *looked* like from the helicopter and after the news people interpreted it as such. But that wasn't true.

The rebels, the lumpen, had just had a very physical brawl with a few dozen LAPD pigs over their manhandling of a fellow by the name of Marc.* During the rebels' battle to free Marc from the pigs' clutches, a radio call came out which instructed the pigs to retreat—to leave the area. They got into their cars and left. *Then* the rebels walked up to Florence Avenue and were attempting to secure the intersection from *all* vehicle traffic—that is: *all vehicle traffic. Any* motorists that attempted to pass had their vehicles bombarded with stones, sticks and bottles. The tactic was to secure the intersection against the eventual return of the LAPD. Which, it must be added, has its 77th Division (a notoriously aggressive and hostile station) right down the avenue of Florence at Broadway. So, the idea, on a purely spur of the moment level, was to secure the main intersection from any and all flowing traffic. What is interesting to note is that the young rebels and lumpen weren't trying to "start" the L.A. Rebellion. And it certainly wasn't about the Rodney King beating or verdict. Though We'd all seen that too, where earlier in that fateful day the four LAPD pigs were acquitted after a trial for the taped beating.†

---

* Marc Williams is the older brother of Damian "Football" Williams, charged in the L.A. 4 case that came out of the beating of Reginald Denny and the securing of the corner of Florence and Normandie. Damian was personally captured by chief of police Daryl Gates in a media staged moment.

† This after they won a change of venue from the city of Los Angeles to Simi Valley where the population is not only amerikan and conservative, but largely inhabited by LAPD members and their families.

LAPD spraypaints one street org's colors over another's, in an attempt to provoke conflict and violence within colonial populations.

While it most definitely wasn't the central factor, it was however one more nail in the coffin of belief in the system. Thus, if only for a few days, while rebels re-appropriated various goods and demolished certain structures they knew were used to exploit and extract wealth out of the area, local, mom and pop shops, were *not* destroyed or looted.

However, by showing over and over the corner of Florence and Normandie, Reginald Denny's stoning, the priest's painting and the chaotic attempts by the rebels and lumpens to secure the corner, the impression of "madness" and "racism" was projected out into the city, region, state and empire. And, of course, like most things involving a challenge to capital, exploitation and private property, the State's propaganda machine put its own spin on these events. With a few agents on the ground in key places, doing whisper campaigns, it wasn't too hard to convince right-wing street (and prison) organizations that it was the "racist blacks attacking Mexicans." Thus began the acrimonious flow of orders to "get even" that issued from the tombs of the SHU units. Check the stats—after the '92 Rebellion, the hoods and barrios across L.A., Watts, Compton and Lynwood erupted in lethal clashes that have culminated in the hostile stand-off that exists today. In the midst of the Rebellion nevertheless, there came a ceasefire order observed by some of the most dangerous and combative street orgs within the New Afrikan communities. Eighty percent of the sets complied with the ceasefire. Bitter enemies blended across color lines in South Central, Watts and Compton. This was in the historic spirit of the 1965 Watts Rebellion[*] that saw a ceasefire and blending of the older New Afrikan street orgs in favor of united action against the LAPD and National Guard. Weed and Seed was intended to prevent this from happening again.

Once the streets orgs agreed upon a ceasefire in 1965, they, unlike the Crips and Bloods of 1992, had a social movement to join as an alternative.[†] A social movement that was increasingly becoming an armed revolution. Malcolm had been

---

[*] The Watts Rebellion began on August 11th and lasted until August 14th. It was brought under control by the state national guard.

[†] This is an important point because from 1965 to at least September 1971, when the Crips began, street org activity was replaced by struggle for liberation within the framework of the Black Liberation Movement. We need only give a cursory glance at who all were street org combatants to point up the power of the BLM then: Alprentice "Bunchy" Carter, Sekou Odinga, Zayd Malik Shakur, Afeni Shakur, Nuh Washington, etc.—all were bangers before joining the revolution. Some in L.A., some in New York or others parts of the empire. The movement attracted them, though, and cadres transformed them. But after the movement was disrupted by the counterrevolutionary thrust of the State—which was, in part, made possible by the movement's own internal weaknesses—street orgs again began to proliferate. So when in '92, the Crips and Bloods agreed on a ceasefire, they had no movement, no cadres to transform them. In swooped Weed and Seed, and the Crips, Bloods and Surenos were easy pickings. It wasn't long before chaos was back as the norm. Only this time as a shooting war between nationals of oppressed nations. A tactic of counterinsurgency is: Problem-Reaction-Solution.

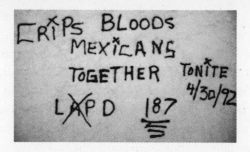

murdered earlier that year, in February. The Revolutionary Action Movement (RAM) was active, and nightly on the bourgeois news, images of civil rights protests were being shown. There existed a more obvious exposure of the fundamental contradiction. New Afrika was being rapidly de-colonized. The system of capitalism was morphing again, looking, searching, for new ways to maintain its control over the internal colonies, while simultaneously struggling to get new colonies in Vietnam, South Amerika and Afrika. The following year, in October, the Black Panther Party for Self-Defense would start, as would the United Slave Organization. Most of the street org combatants who'd come together in a ceasefire during the 1965 Watts Rebellion would go on to join either the Panther Party or the United Slaves. A move that wasn't lost on the FBI who, thru its Counterintelligence Program (COINTELPRO), worked tirelessly to exacerbate pre-existing conflicts between individual combatants that inevitably spilled over into gunfights and murders.[*]

The same tactics were used against the Crips and Bloods under Weed and Seed, after the 1992 Rebellion. Same war, same objective, different names for the maneuvers. What should come across as evident to us as We reflect on the various tactics used

---

[*] See: John Potash, *The FBI War on Tupac Shakur & Black Leaders* (Progressive Left Press, 2007).

against us over the centuries is that the enemy has more faith in our ability to get free than We do. Put another way, the enemy has had to implement so many ploys, to hold, control, exploit and now to eliminate us, that for us to sit and point these things out makes even the most astute observer appear as a wingnut conspiracy theorist. Though of course, it's no theory when it's actually happening; as Butch Lee and J. Sakai have pointed out, it ain't a conspiracy when it's done outright and in the open—it's a *strategy*. Why else would the imperialists have to implement plan after plan—sometimes elaborate and varied—to contain New Afrika (or any other colony) if (1) it wasn't capable of breaking free, (2) it wasn't an asset, and (3) it wasn't able to turn it's oppression into the actual defeat of the empire itself?*

Oftentimes the reaction to an issue can be a lesson unto itself. In this instance the enemy's reaction to our very existence is quite enough for those paying attention, to recognize the vast potential in our collective ability to break de chains. Of course, the fact remains that the chains which bind—that at this stage are psychological—are so thoroughly in place that the masses have to be *convinced* that they are oppressed. Consciousness will

---

* To "Capitalism as We know it to be, in present & past form. Which is to say that, no matter the internal struggles in Europe, among Europeans, between those who ruled & those who were ruled, between serfs & lords, etc.—no matter these influences—what cemented & gave assurance to the development of what We know as capitalism, imperialism, was the enslavement & transport of Afrikan people, *from* the Afrikan to other continents. Was the circumstances which led to the birth of New Afrika. The movement of Afrikan people *from* independence—*to* independence, is what will end the life of the empire. No matter how hard it may be for some folks to accept right now." Bakari Shanna, *Notes From A New Afrikan P.O.W. Journal, Book Two* (Spear & Shield Publications, 1978).

not fall from the sky. Nor will people be moved to action by mere thoughts or ideas in anyone's head. On both counts, material, earthbound, tangibles—food, clothing, shelter, land, and control of destiny (socialism)—will motivate the masses. People are moved by interests.*

So, in closing, it never was about Rodney King, the verdict, or any singular thing at all. These, however were accelerants, or sparks, at any given time, but the basic most fundamental thing that causes us to struggle, to resist, is that We are not collectively free to determine our own destiny. That We are under the thumb of u.s. imperialism. And this imperialism is administered thru colonialism—colonial violence (both armed and unarmed). Violence does damage (physically or mentally) in the streets and in the schools. Thru police shootings or cultural hegemony. The colonialism is in place to exploit us through capitalism. Let's be clear on this. Because whether the people are conscious of this or not, it is the reality We are in. And it follows that it will be our recognition, challenge to and resolution of this fundamental contradiction that will end our national oppression. Without overstanding this, We'll continue to be played on amerika's ferris wheel of "citizenry"—dazed and confused. Being led by the "black" bourgeoisie to meekly just "get along" with our oppression. Hau!

---

* It used to be that "raising consciousness" to particular levels was enough to show the masses that no real self-determination existed and that bourgeois democracy was a sham. Now, however, with the initiative firmly in the clutches of the State, globalists and their propagandists and cadre, We have to literally *convince* the masses that all this is smoke and mirrors. It's a daunting task, actually. Especially in the post-9/11 age of "everyone who is anti-State is a terrorist." Still, however, it is what has to be done.

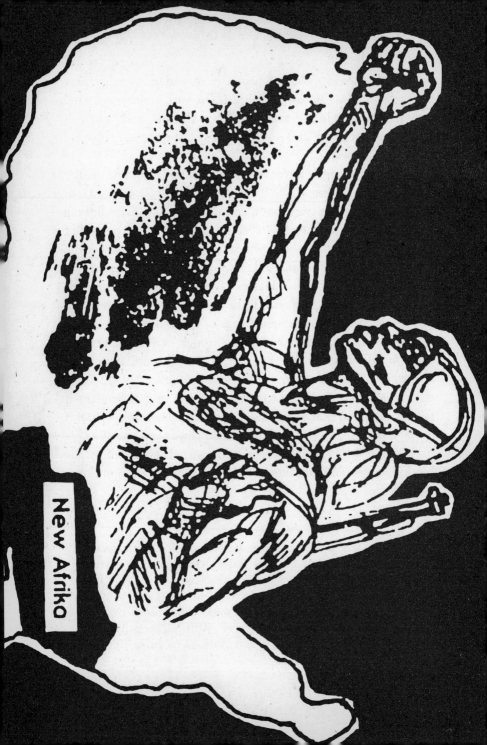

New Afrika

Get Up For The Down Stroke

A response to: Black Liberation in the 21st Century: A Revolutionary Reassessment of Black Nationalism[*]

Part One

> *There's never been a "question" for us, only a task, a goal: the struggle to <u>regain</u> our independence as a separate people with interests which oppose those of the empire. A goal for us, is a "question" for those outside the nation who have a different nationality, and/or for those inside the nation who have a different ideology, e.g., the phrase "national question" was coined by people trying to determine what position they would take regarding the struggle of colonized peoples—there was never a "national question" for the colonized themselves.*[†]

---

[*] Kevin Rashid Johnson, "Black Liberation in the 21st Century: A Revolutionary Reassessment of Black Nationalism." This essay first appeared in *Right On!* #19, Spring 2010, and was subsequently reprinted on a number of websites. It can be found online at http://rashidmod.com/?p=301

[†] Atiba Shanna, "On What It Means to 'Re-Build'," p. 29.

51

Sometimes in the course of struggle, whether around theory, philosophy, ideology or tactics, We get tangled, as it were, in ideas so contradictory and muddled that We hardly have the ability to overstand how We reached that point, let alone how to extricate ourselves from it. We'll often allow such confusion to actually become us, or so We think, and then any critique of the confusion is seen as a personal critique of ourselves rather than an honest and revolutionary attempt to disentangle oneself from ideo-theoretical muck and mire. This is one of the things We're confronted by in the New Afrikan Black Panther Party-Prison Chapter's (NABPP) position on the so-called "national question."

What a mind-blowing tangle of ideo-theoretical mumbo-jumbo this piece/position is. There appears to have been some effort put forth early on to position themselves on an objective plane, for what it's worth, but that evaporated immediately as the tools they were using to excavate the "facts" faltered and, eventually, altogether broke apart in the process of their reasoning. The results were a pathetic attempt at continuing on in spite of having not a fact to stand on.

We find it a bit odd, or perhaps not so at all, that in the NABPP's piece to supposedly refute, or ideologically combat, the New Afrikan Independence Movement's (NAIM) position on land—specifically our National Territory—that they'd not use one actual quote of a New Afrikan revolutionary nationalist. And while at the outset they mention the Provisional Government of the Republic of New Afrika (PG-RNA), the New Afrikan People's Organization (NAPO), the New Afrikan Maoist Party (NAMP) and the Maoist Internationalist Movement (MIM), they fail to post their positions. What the NABPP does is use everyone except those whose position they are refuting to bolster their position. And throughout their position piece they do what exactly? They attempt to prove that New Afrikans are:

→ A people without a need for a National Territory.

→ A nation within a nation but requiring no self-determination.

→ A nation which, when it exerts its need for land of its own, is somehow separatist and by implication "racist."

→ A people who, in order to get free, must wait on and then unite with the citizens of the oppressor nation.

→ And finally, that We are sadly misled by our strategies, which according to the NABPP no longer have any basis for existence.

Of course, in a magnificent feat of ideological gymnastics they switch at one point and say that amerikans are so thoroughly anti-New-Afrikan (citing the response to the Katrina disaster/strategy of depopulation) that our strategy should be to unite with them to keep things from "almost certainly degenerating into an imperialist-sponsored race war." So in this baffling projection those We must unite with to get free are simultaneously those who will "almost certainly" annihilate us in "an imperialist-sponsored race war."

We are not amused in the least by the hodgepodge of ideological-theoretical claptrap in question. Nor are We altogether surprised. After all, this is a group called the New Afrikan Black Panther Party-Prison Chapter. We have always been struck by this, since it is such a redundancy, such an obvious rip-off and regrafting of... Well, We'll save all that for another time. Let's go on and get into the quicksand mess of this position and work our way thru in the hopes of this being a teachable moment. And while We'd like to think that this would help dis-entangle the NABPP from its muddle, We seriously doubt that will be the case, since it never really seemed to want to struggle *with* the NAIM on this point. Only *against* us.

As We carry on, We too will use quotes, passages and points of authority to frame certain things or to flesh out positions—though We will use those best qualified to inform the arguments We use. We won't go get Chairman Mao to instruct us on New Afrikan social development. While We do in fact revere Chairman Mao and have always studied the works of the Chinese Communist Party and the People's Revolution, We feel it best to use our own ideologues to make our own points. And We most certainly will not be using anything from old imperialist Stalin. He may be looked upon as a "comrade" by the NABPP, but not by us.

We opened this response with a quote by Comrad-Brother Owusu Yaki Yakubu, an erstwhile member of the Coordinating Committee of the Black Liberation Army, the New Afrikan Prisoners Organization, the Provisional Government of the Republic of New Afrika, and of the Spear and Shield Collective. Comrad-Brother Yaki is perhaps one of our keenest ideologues and theoreticians and will be quoted at length here, for it was some of his contributions, along with those of other Comrads in the PG-RNA and NAPO, that were largely responsible for kick-starting the resurgence of the NAIM today. Their words and ideas are as worthy as Chairman Mao is to us.

We had taken for granted that the NABPP-PC was an organization in the NAIM because it uses in its name our national identity.

We overstand and do, to a great extent, anticipate that our national identity—New Afrikan—will take root and evolve into the dominant name used by our people. We feel this because it is a *correct idea* that projects our aspirations. And, with the mass usage of this will eventually, inevitably, come various class divisions and aspirations. It's much like when, in the early and mid-1960s, the young Black Liberation Movement (BLM), as led by

Malcolm X and the Revolutionary Action Movement (RAM), began to use "black" in place of "negro" to symbolize and embody not only an objective change in external projection, but also a subjective change of internal dynamics. Which is to say, the BLM was decidedly nationalist and about self-determination. While it saw the civil rights movement as integrationist (bourgeois nationalist) and neo-colonial.

Though Malcolm would always make the distinction between a "black" person and a "negro," he'd also let the people know that they shouldn't be fooled by the term negro and that it was, in fact, a colonialist-manufactured tool. Thus, he'd always say, "the so-called negro." That is, *so-called* by the oppressor and then used by the unknowing (colonial subjects), and/or by the *aware* (collaborators), to realize their class interests. Eventually the term "negro" got phased out as the "black" masses exerted themselves and demanded to be dealt with on terms of their own deciding. Of course, it goes without saying that while it was, at that time in our social development, necessary to distinguish "black" (nationalist) from "negro" (integrationist)—as a sense of coming into our own, it wasn't sufficient. It wasn't a politically or ideologically sound platform to stand on or from which to launch and sustain a national liberation revolution.

The first people using the radical term "black" were, by and large, about essentially the same thing: a sense of self, separate of and determined by our own internal dynamics and informed by objective reality in a dialectical materialist way. National liberation struggles were raging all across the planet. So, as things were perceived at that particular time and in that space, "black" was an idea whose time had come.

We are approaching that time now in our consciousness. The masses—of all the internal and external colonies—are beginning to stir. Settlers and citizens of the oppressor nations, those in the metropole, are beginning to stir as well. Prisoners across the empire are in the early stages of unity and rebellion (again) as focus is trained on ways to get free, and this is but the beginning. Thus, when We saw this organization, the NABPP-PC, come onto the scene and read bits and pieces of its work here and there, We instinctively mistook their usage of "New Afrikan" to mean they were a revolutionary nationalist group aligned with the constellation of organizations within the NAIM. Because, you see, to call oneself *New Afrikan*, at this early stage, is to be, by and large, about what We in the NAIM are about: *Land*, *Independence* and *Socialism*. What We find, however, with the publishing of its position on the so-called "national question," is that it's really about a "multi-ethnic, multi-racial socialist amerika"; i.e., radical integration.

In other words, it does not see the Provisional Government (People's Center Council, People's Revolutionary Leadership Council, New Afrikan Security Forces, etc.) as the State-in-exile of the Republic of New Afrika. It is not sworn to the Code of Umoja (the New Afrikan National Constitution); it has no pledge to the New Afrikan Creed, nor does it recognize the New Afrikan Declaration of Independence. And We know this because these are the official documents/instruments that We in the NAIM stand on and utilize to realize our national independence struggle for self-determination and liberation of our National Territory in the Kush (New Afrika).

"For us," as Comrad-Brother Yaki so eloquently said, *"there was never a national question."* That, he said, was "for those inside the nation who have a *different* ideology."* (our emphasis)

We thought that by the NABPP-PC calling itself "New Afrikan" that it was in compliance with Article I, Section 7, of the Code of Umoja which states:

---

* Ibid.

> *All citizens of the Republic of New Afrika who are aware of*
> *their citizenship are conscious New Afrikan citizens.*

Though, to be fair, Section 7, in Article I, is preceded by Section 1:

> *Each Afrikan person born in America is a citizen of the*
> *Republic of New Afrika.*

And Section 2:

> *Any child born to a citizen of the Republic of New Afrika is*
> *a citizen of the Republic of New Afrika.*

Those aware, We call "conscious citizens." Those not knowing are
referred to as "unconscious citizens." The unconscious citizens
never use "New Afrikan" because they are, as of yet, unaware of
it. So, this is how We got confused by the NABPP-PC.

Section 3 of Article I says:

> *Any person not otherwise a citizen of the Republic of New*
> *Afrika may become a citizen of the Republic of New Afrika*
> *by completing the procedures for naturalization as pro-*
> *vided by the People's Center Council.*

We'll come back to Article I, Section 3, of the Code of Umoja, as
We go on to combat the NABPP's distortion of the NAIM as "black
separatists." Though as anyone can see, by the first line of Section
3, this can't be the case. But let's move on. Dig this:

> *Who are We, those of us who built a national "black" pris-*
> *oners organization? There is much evidence to show that as*
> *each day passes, more and more "black" prisoners identify*
> *themselves as New Afrikans and work on behalf of the*
> *New Afrikan Independence Movement. Despite the ques-*
> *tions many of us may raise concerning them, two of the*
> *things which define our movement and guide it, are the*

New Afrikan Declaration of Independence and the New Afrikan Creed. Our Declaration of Independence states, in part, that We, "in consequence of our inextinguishable determination to go a different way, to build a new and better world, do hereby declare ourselves free and independent of the jurisdiction of the united states of amerika and the obligations which that country's unilateral decision to make our ancestors and ourselves paper citizens placed on us."

When We pledge ourselves to the New Afrikan Creed, We do so with the belief that "the fundamental reason our oppression continues is that We, as a people, lack the power to control our lives," and that the fundamental way to gain that power and end oppression, is to build a sovereign black nation.

We are guided by the strategic objective of winning sovereignty for our nation, to build a new, socialist society, and to "support and wage the world revolution until all people everywhere are so free" (New Afrikan Declaration of Independence). If an organization is to be built by those who identify themselves as New Afrikans, whether a national ("black") prisoners organization, or a national and/or local ("black") students, or tenants organization, it must rest on a foundation of the New Afrikan Declaration of Independence and the New Afrikan Creed. These are integral parts of our ideo-framework, and it's upon this foundation that all else rests—unity included.

---

* Notes From A New Afrikan P.O.W. Journal, Book #3, Mbili Shanna, Spear and Shield Publications.

The National "Question"

Let's fall into the NABPP's position on the so-called "national question." Which is really *not* what the piece is actually about because the national question (as originally debated) was primarily about whether New Afrikans actually comprised a nation within a nation here. The NABPP concedes that We do, in fact, comprise a nation within the political borders of the empire. That's not their beef. Their beef boils down to whether We actually are sound in our struggle for land in the National Territory. Our efforts to Free The Land are critiqued, while in the same breath the NABPP-PC advocates the taking of all the land in the empire for a "multi-ethnic, multi-racial, socialist amerika." Essentially, a new and improved (reformed) amerika.

This so-called "Reassessment of Black Nationalism" (to use their subtitle) is nothing more than their propagation of radical integration in drag as a "deepened" version of Huey P. Newton's analysis on intercommunalism. The facts of this will easily bear out as We go forward. Pay close attention. Their position paper on the so-called "national question" could very well have been titled "The Nation that Needs No Land," or "Soon Whitey Comes To Help." At times it's actually *that* pitiful in its shameless hat-in-hand plea for oppressor-nation citizens to "save the day." In one astounding admission of blind hope and child-like idealism, they say that uniting with settler radicals is a step towards uniting all of humanity and "the whole world becoming one people." But let us not get ahead of ourselves here. We must proceed with caution because this can really raise consciousness.

The opening shots are fired at the Black Belt Thesis (BBT) as developed by Harry Haywood, who was first a member of the African Blood Brotherhood (one of many points the NABPP fails to mention in this piece—this is called deception by omission), and then of the settler Communist Party-USA. In fact, the whole African Blood Brotherhood (ABB) was incorporated into the CPUSA, which effectively *liquidated* the first actual New Afrikan Communist Organization:

> It was founded in 1919 at the same time as the first
> Vietnamese communist study groups and the Chinese
> Communist Party. Yet some forty years later, in a new
> generation of struggle, New Afrikans once again faced the
> necessity of building a communist center from ground zero.[*]

Why, in fact, was this, that in the 1960s, "New Afrikans had to start building a communist center from ground zero"? Because our first communist organization found it expedient to unite in the same organization (and under its leadership), with settlers who did not share our national interests—no matter what they said to the contrary. Harry Haywood's so-called "Black Belt Thesis" was doomed from the outset and here's why:

---

[*] E. Tani and Kae Sera, *False Nationalism, False Internationalism: Contradictions in the Armed Struggle*, (Seeds Beneath The Snow, 1985), pp. 45–46.

> *We can say that, whether knowingly or not, the CPUSA*
> *served the interests of U.S. Imperialism by: 1) leading the*
> *oppressed <u>away</u> from armed struggle, <u>away</u> from joining*
> *the world revolution. 2) Convincing people that <u>national</u>*
> *<u>liberation</u> and communism were opposed to each other.*
> *3) Using Third World "communists" to <u>disunite</u> the op-*
> *pressed nations, while also placing the activities of the*
> *oppressed under constant monitoring and meddling of*
> *euro-amerikans. "Left" settlerism worked as a counter-*
> *revolutionary police for the empire. And their most loyal*
> *Third World "communists" become "<u>unconscious traitors</u>"*
> *to their own people.* (our emphasis)*

The term "Black Belt" entered the national lexicon, however, and
came to denote the actual contiguous string of New Afrikan dominated counties—fifty in all—that stretched from the Louisiana
Delta to the Atlantic Ocean. But Harry Haywood's BBT played
but a small, nominal, part in our later designation, in 1968, of
Louisiana, Mississippi, Alabama, Georgia and South Carolina as
the New Afrikan National Territory. We didn't need no BBT to
inform us where our nationals were. Where We labored, fought,
died and buried our ancestors. We knew where "down home" was.

> *[The NABPP] fails to mention the small fact that the rea-*
> *son the 1960s revolutionary struggle produced national-*
> *ism and separatism is because the masses of oppressed in*
> *the struggle themselves demanded it. And wouldn't have*
> *it any other way. It wasn't because Harry Haywood's*
> *writing was reprinted in 1979 or because someone got an*
> *idea about Black ideological nationalism. Saying that is*
> *complete b.s., only oppressor thinking. It was all those in*

---

* Ibid., p. 46.

*struggle themselves who demanded political separation—
who forced white civil rights workers out of the movement,
who started all-New Afrikan initiatives, projects and organizations. This surge was particularly sharp because of
the years of bitter experience, which led to activists becoming tired of euro-settler leftists and liberals intervening
in their relationships, manipulating them, lying to them,
attempting to stay their rulers with honeyed words and
money. Talk about neo-colonialism, there it was.* [*]

But again, We contend that the NABPP's attack on this position
is but a smokescreen masking their true intent. We notice the
ideological deficiencies bleeding thru almost immediately as the
NABPP can't seem to decide whether We, as a people, are New
Afrikans or "blacks." It slips easily back and forth in a dizzying
array of ideo-theoretical schizophrenia as it attempts to discred-
it the land requirement/objective of the NAIM, with old tenets
which actually have nothing to do with us. We think the NABPP
is studying other material and heaping its analysis of that work
onto us.

Had the NABPP been studying the body of work produced
by cadres of the NAIM they'd have known early on that our struggle for national liberation (Land, Independence and Socialism)
has nothing to do with any Black Belt Thesis, Harry Haywood
or the CPUSA/Comintern. We don't import ideas. And while
the NABPP calls its position paper "Black Liberation in the 21st
Century: A Revolutionary Reassessment of Black Nationalism,"
We in the NAIM "reassessed" so-called "black nationalism" in
the *20th century*. The exhaustion of so-called "black" nationalism
was done with the collapse of the Black Liberation Movement
(BLM) and reassessed, in a scientific manner, as the New Afrikan

---

[*] Internal communication with an elder Comrad.

Independence Movement. We are not "black" nationalists. We are not about "black" liberation. We are revolutionary New Afrikan nationalists and We are about New Afrikan Independence (Land and Socialism). Had the NABPP been studying *our* material they'd have easily known this. We don't base our struggle on the false social construction of "race" or color. We are anti-racists. At one point in this so-called "revolutionary reassessment" the NABPP calls the NAIM the "black movement." A deliberate distortion of our struggle. We resent this. We are the ones who led the ideological struggle for the usage of New Afrikan as our national identity (nationality) over "black" as a racial identity.

In fact, check out the wise words of Comrad-Brother Yaki:

> *The de-construction of "race" as a concept and the struggle against racism on the political front starts by understanding "politics" as everything related to our lives, and not just those things related to the electoral arena. More precisely, We can define politics as a concentrated expression of economics, concerned with the acquisition, retention and use of state power, which is used to realize revolutionary interests of society. Politically, the de-construction of "race" attacks the cause, and seeks to prevent the use of "race" to disguise it.*

The NAIM is not about "black" nationalism as the NABPP mistakenly postulates, and it is precisely because We are not about "black" nationalism, or an ambiguously defined "liberation," that for us there is no "national question." Nor is there one pertaining to our requirement for land. We are a nation, nations require land to administer the needs of their nationals. It's not a complicated thing, really.

---

* Sayles, p. 330.

National Reality

We call into question the material ("tools") the NABPP is using to make its "revolutionary reassessment" since it appears to us that they are hardly talking about New Afrikans. For instance, they refer to colonized New Afrikans as a "rural peasantry." This is a term used by Russian and Chinese comrades when describing their nationals—in their assessment of their people. Another ill-fitting graft is tied onto New Afrikan social development in order to disguise the obvious weak points and glaring errors in perception. There was no feudalism here. The NABPP says the...

> ... *Black population within the U.S. is no longer a rural peasantry. It is overwhelmingly a proletarian nation (wage slaves) dispersed across the U.S. and concentrated in and around urban centers in predominantly Black or multi-ethnic oppressed communities.* [*]

Aside from the ideological muddle of terms like "black" and "multi-ethnic" (as if this were Yugoslavia—or worse, one "United

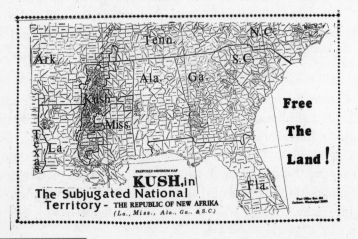

PROPOSED MINIMUM MAP
KUSH,in
The Subjugated National
Territory - THE REPUBLIC OF NEW AFRIKA
(La., Miss., Ala., Ga., & S.C.)

Free
The
Land!

Post Office Box 465
Jackson, Mississippi 39205

---

[*] Johnson.

States" with just a few "multi-ethnics" inside) the NABPP totally misses the boat on the fact that colonized Afrikans, who evolved into New Afrikans here, were stolen to be used as a permanent proletariat. The New Afrikan nation was born as a working-class nation of permanent proletarians. The fact that We weren't paid does not preclude the fact that We were workers. What do they think so-called "slavery" (colonialism) entails if not work?

> Afrikans were the landless, propertyless, permanent work-ers of the U.S. Empire. They were not just slaves—the Afrikan nation as a whole served as a proletariat for the Euro-Amerikan oppressor nation. The Afrikan colony sup-ported on its shoulders the building of Euro-Amerikan society more "prosperous," more "egalitarian" and yes, more "democratic" than any in semi-feudal Old Europe... Amerika imported a proletariat from Afrika, a proletariat permanently chained in an internal colony, laboring for the benefit of all settlers. Afrikan workers might be individ-ually owned, like tools and draft animals, by some settlers and not others, but in their colonial subjugation they were as a whole owned by the entire Euro-Amerikan nation.*

The NABPP says We were "dispersed" across the u.s. and it is in fact this "dispersal" out of the National Territory that they go on to use as their basis for our requirement of land being "outmod-ed." That the so-called "Black Belt Thesis" (which We don't use) is no longer relevant because We no longer make up the majority in the National Territory. What a shallow analysis. Yeah, this is really a deepened analysis here, huh? There are more Irish people in the u.s. than there are in Ireland—does this mean they have no claim to, or need for, a national territory? And what of the

---

* Sakai, p. 9.

Kanaka Maoli, the Indigenous of Hawaii, who've been drastically decimated by settlerism to the point where they are but a fraction of their former selves? What of the Basque?

Our migration out of the National Territory and into amerika was akin to any other oppressed people who, having their own territory mangled and ravished by encroaching capitalism, went in search of sustenance—work to feed, clothe and house themselves. To feel safe and stable—to survive in the tradewinds of a hostile imperialism. We came up outta the National Territory as refugees. Much like Mexicanos and other destitute peoples from Central and South Amerika, who've been NAFTA'd into mass migrations for survival. Our nationals, too, sent remittances "back home" to family members still in the Kush. We *still* listened to Down Home Blues, or Southern Gospel, had fish fry's and did what We do while in amerika. And our parents would send us *home* for the summer to be with "Big Momma," "Nana," "Aunt Lilly" and our cousins who'd never left the National Territory. Our nationals who left (to go up North, back East and out West):

> They were <u>refugees</u>, those who "migrated" from the
> National Territory during the WWI and WWII years.
> Our elders were <u>refugees</u> during the years of the "Black
> Codes" when they fled the National Territory. The cities
> of amerika were full of New Afrikan refugees who entered
> them during the '30s, '40s, escaping the Klan and the
> southern prison. One step ahead of the hounds, a few min-
> utes ahead of the lynch mob is how many New Afrikans
> came North. Refugees from the National Territory.*

---

* Sayles, p. 104.

66

The NABPP claims to have "deepened" the analysis put forward by Huey P. Newton of the "original" Black Panther Party.[*] They also claim to have reached this "deepened" state by employing the philosophical tools of dialectical materialism. Hmmm... Surprisingly, We too have used these same philosophical tools to reach our conclusions on the land issue. Which can easily stand up in objective reality, i.e., the criterion of truth.

While the NABPP claims to have "deepened" the analysis put forward by Huey P. Newton, there certainly appears to be no such deepening of any such analysis in this position paper. If anything, it's a distortion of Huey P. Newton's analysis and a grafting on of non-applicable realities that point more to *confusion* than to any real breakthrough or "deepened" analysis. Seriously, is it *deeper* that We are a "nation within a nation"? Or is it *deeper*

---

[*] Contrary to what the NABPP says about Huey P. Newton being of the original Black Panther Party, the fact of the matter is Huey P. Newton and Bobby Seale founded the third organization calling itself the Black Panther Party. The first usage of the panther as a symbol for a political party was done by the Lowndes County Freedom Organization, formed by the Student Non-Violent Coordinating Committee (SNCC) in the National Territory (Alabama)—"It was a New Afrikan electoral alternative to the regular Democratic Party doing voter registration gun in hand and running for county offices." The second organization to use the panther was the Revolutionary Action Movement (RAM) which began to, "Use the black panther symbol and start Black Panther Parties in the northern New Afrikan ghettoes. Local BPP offices were set up in New York, Cleveland, Philadelphia, San Francisco and other cities." The BPP that Huey P. Newton and Bobby Seale would found would actually be the third organization calling itself the Black Panther Party and would, in fact, have to distinguish itself by putting "For Self-Defense" on its name. And while there were great differences between these organizations, the point is that the original BPP was founded in Lowndes County, Alabama. (See: Tani and Sera, pp. 175–176.)

that they are referring to empire-builder Stalin as "comrade"? Is it *deeper* that New Afrikans are referred to as a "rural peasantry"? Or is it *deeper* that "black" nationalism is no longer applicable? Is it *deeper* that euro-amerikans are said to be the key to the "liberation of humanity and the whole world becoming one people"? Wake us up when it *really* gets deep will you?

The NABPP is attempting to view New Afrikan social development through the socio-political lens of 1930s China or 1940s Russia. Instead of critically applying the tools of dialectical materialism to reach the truth, as it is, they are blowing dialectical materialist smoke, while lazily placing over the top of New Afrika, vis-a-vis the u.s. empire, a Chinese or Russian *political* lens. What's being touted as a philosophical conclusion, reached through the application of dialectical materialism, is actually a slow-witted political *graft*. We know this because not one thing in this whole piece is *new* or the result of any "deepened" analysis. The NABPP says that our struggle for the National Territory is hopelessly wrong, or as they put it:

> ... *outmoded ideas and formulations that no longer fit the current situation.*

When did a National Territory, the landbase of a nation(ality), become "outmoded"? They say this, then go right along to say, it's necessary to lead a "multi-ethnic, multi-racial" struggle for a "socialist amerika"—where, on the moon? No... on this land—a National Territory, dig?

Watch your step, please, the inconsistencies and contradictions are all over the place. There *is* some "idealism" going on here, but it's wholly manufactured and promoted by the NABPP.

The NABPP, when compiling this position paper, would have fared much better We think in reaching this so-called "deepened" analysis, had they studied our (New Afrikans') social development as documented by cadres of the New Afrikan Independence Movement. We have a vast body of ideo-theoretical work. We are reminded here of a masterstroke of constructive criticism delivered to the reactionary African Peoples Socialist Party (APSP), on practically the same points We now find the NABPP postulating, by Comrad-Brother Chokwe Lumumba, Chairman of the New Afrikan Peoples Organization.[*] Truly a teachable/learning moment. We feel the NABPP would do well to check the actual foundations upon which the NAIM stands before venturing to critique us based on what's "believed" to be our position from the 1930s.

National Liberation or Radical Integration

The whole title of the NABPP's position paper is a false flag distortion of what's actually on the table here. Well, either that or the NABPP is simply dull.

"Black Liberation in the 21st Century: A Revolutionary Reassessment of Black Nationalism"—that's the whole title. Pretty lofty, huh? The thing is, though, the NABPP uses the word "_black_" perhaps over 22 times in describing New Afrikans—who they claim to recognize as a nation—so, this would mean... that it's a "black nation"? So, in their "revolutionary reassessment" *of*

---

[*] Chokwe Lumumba, *Roots of the New Afrikan Independence Movement*.

"black nationalism" they can't seem to extricate themselves or "deepen" their "analysis" enough to stop using the socially constructed binary terms of "race"? Watch your step, please. See, this is what We mean about a false flag, a distortion. It's not now nor has it really ever been about "a revolutionary reassessment of black nationalism." No, this is about radical integration. Which, of course, is not *new* and is certainly not the result of a "deepened" analysis. Let us share something that *We* laid out in *1988*:

> *In terms of re-orientation, the movement must adjust to objective reality and establish new principles (or to reinforce old ones). For instance, We ain't calling ourselves a "civil rights movement" or an ambiguously defined "Black Power" or "Black Liberation" movement. We ain't adopting lines from the CPUSA and saying We gonna form United Fronts Against Fascism, which the BPP did under the leadership of Huey P. Newton and Bobby Seale. Nor are We adopting lines from the Trots and saying We gonna establish a "black dictatorship" in amerika.*
>
> *The line for this stage says We're waging a New Afrikan national liberation revolution, i.e. It's a struggle for national independence and socialism.*

The NABPP is posturing as if it is somehow involved in some great new debate about the insufficiency of "black" nationalism as a strategy for freedom. It further propagates this erroneous subtitle of a "revolutionary reassessment" as if it has somehow made a "miraculous breakthrough"—a great leap forward—in some "deepened analysis" about why our position on the National

---

* Atiba Shanna, "Notes on Cadre Policy and Development," *Vita Wa Watu: New Afrikan Theoretical Journal, Book #12*, April 1988, p. 10.

Territory is "outmoded." Why, in fact, We need no land, even though We are a nation. You wanna know, really, how new this is? This is what pig president Thomas Jefferson said, as offered by Professor Peter S. Onuf:

> He did know, with as much certainty as his own experience and observation could authorize that [New Afrikan] slaves constituted a distinct nation. The crimes against slaves therefore had to be understood first in national terms [...] Virginia slaves were a people without a country, a captive nation...*

Not only had We become a "distinct nation," but We had human rights, as well. And, with the 13th Amendment to the u.s. Constitution, in 1865, We'd been given land under Field Order No. 15. But this was too much like right, so at the same time as New Afrika was granted its freedom with the 13th Amendment, the imperialists doubled back on us and made the unilateral (single, without our consent) decision to make us "paper citizens"— that is, citizens on paper only—with the 14th Amendment. This Amendment reversed Field Order No. 15 which gave us land for our free nation and with it they said essentially, "Now, you don't need any separate land for yourselves—you're citizens: all this land is yours!"

And this is what the NABPP is saying as well. While it claims to recognize that New Afrikans are a "distinct nation," it advocates that We forego any struggle for our own land, for self-determination, in a Socialist Republic of New Afrika, and that instead We should unite with the settler citizens (like the liquidated African Blood Brotherhood did) and struggle in a "multi-ethnic,

---

* Peter S. Onuf, *Jefferson's Empire: The Language of American Nationhood*, (University Press of Virginia, 2000), pp. 148–149.

multi-racial" way for a "socialist amerika." Radical integration, We repeat, is not new.

Contrary to the erroneous claim made by the NABPP about our struggle for land being based on the Black Belt Thesis of Harry Haywood, We have to say that We stand firm, instead, on the Precepts of the New Afrikan Creed, Number 7:

> I believe in the Malcolm X Doctrine: that We must organize upon this land, and hold a plebiscite, to tell the world by vote that We are free and the land independent, and that, after the vote, We must stand ready to defend ourselves establishing the Nation beyond contradiction. (Changes approved May 5, 1991—People's Center Council).

There's nothing in our documents about any BBT, or Harry Haywood. Here's the thing: amerika is a prisonhouse of nations, and no matter how much distortion is applied to this reality, it ain't going away. This is an empire. It is as much an empire as Stalin's USSR was. Whole nations are submerged under the grand illusion of a "United States," just as it was under the grand illusion of a Union of Soviet Socialist Republics. People We never knew existed were under there—denied their national independence. Subjugated, colonized and politically distorted. And here We find in this piece the NABPP saying:

> National "Liberation" has therefore proved empty of substance to oppressed Third World peoples, absent the defeat of imperialism, just as it would in a struggle for New Afrikan national "liberation" in the Southern U.S. territory absent the defeat of imperialism. Moreover, any such struggle would almost certainly degenerate into an imperialist-sponsored race war, similar to what went down in the Kosovo conflict.

We're not altogether sure why they chose to put "liberation" in scare quotes, since the word alone only means freedom and carries no political connotations, but that's pretty indicative of this whole so-called "reassessment" position. The lack of consciousness is evident here where they begin by saying "National Liberation has therefore proved empty..." Now, forgive us if We seem a little slow here on the uptake, but what—We wonder—would be the result of "... leading the whole working class," as the NABPP says in another part of this piece, "and the broad masses in pulling down the capitalist-imperialist system and achieving social justice for all," if, not _national liberation_?? It would be National Liberation of/for a "multi-ethnic, multi-racial socialist amerika." And that, dear reader, is the rub—radical integration. Pay lip service to New Afrikans being a nation, but actively block our struggle for self-determination, while promoting a "multi-ethnic, multi-racial socialist amerika." Stalin, whom the NABPP refers to as "Comrade J.V. Stalin," would be proud. Hey, and if the submerged nations begin to struggle you all can simply exile us some place, right?

Since when has fighting for national liberation become "empty" to Third World people? Did the ETA get that memo? We in the New Afrikan People's Liberation Army sure as hell didn't. We don't think the EZLN or Macheteros got that one either. Here's the thing, there are two types of nationalism: revolutionary nationalism and bourgeois nationalism. Check out what Huey Newton himself had to say:

> There are two kinds of nationalism: revolutionary national-
> ism, and reactionary nationalism. Revolutionary national-
> ism is dependent upon a people's revolution with the end
> result being the people in power. Therefore, to be a revo-
> lutionary nationalist you would by necessity have to be a

socialist. If you are a reactionary nationalist, you are not a
socialist, and your goal is the oppression of the people.[*]

The NAIM is a revolutionary nationalist movement. Our nationality is New Afrikan. Our nation is called the Republic of New Afrika. Our National Territory lies in the southeast quadrant of North Amerika. Ours is a war of national liberation. That's our get down: Land, Independence and Socialism.

So, in spite of the NABPP posturing against our revolutionary nationalism, they are nationalists themselves. They just want a "Socialist Amerika"—still a nation—of a "multi-ethnic, multi-racial" character. That's called *radical integration*.

Let's be clear: For the whole Third World the NABPP has reached the conclusion that "National Liberation is empty of substance absent the defeat of imperialism..." We better hurry and get this memo out to all the Third World national liberation struggles: "NO USE IN TRYING, IT'S NOT GOING TO WORK! GO HOME, YOU HAVEN'T A CHANCE IN HELL!"

See how *crazy* that sounds? We can't make this stuff up, folks.

The Oppressor Nation
As We said before, the u.s. is an empire, under which is submerged many nations. Both internally and externally the u.s. casts its pall over the lives of millions in a neo-colonial relationship so refined and perfected that the masses themselves eagerly campaign for

---

[*] Huey Newton. "Huey Newton Talks to the Movement About the Black Panther Party, Cultural Nationalism, SNCC, Liberals and White Revolutionaries," in Philip S. Foner ed., *The Black Panthers Speak*, (Cambridge, MA: Da Capo Press, 2002), p. 50.

and work in support of their own oppression. All to the squealing delight of the bourgeoisie. And the settler citizens of the empire, who have always been loyal to their ruling class against all forms of struggle which genuinely push for real revolutionary change, are right there with them reaping the benefits of empire.

The settlers don't mark their wealth by the accumulation of ideas—that's fool's gold to them. They *got* their freedom, or so they think (which is arguable), they ain't going to unite with a movement that puts their "things" in jeopardy. The NABPP can run from suburb to suburb trying to organize some "multi-ethnic, multi-racial" mass and they'll be debating with IRA accounts, 401ks, car notes and retirement plans. What better lives could the settlers hope for? Their bread is buttered on the side that holds loyalty to the empire.

This has proven true even of the settlers calling themselves "communists." The CPUSA has a sickening history of collaboration with empire against oppressed nations. False nationalism and false internationalism are not new phenomena. We are not against alliances with genuine revolutionaries and We *are* internationalists, however We are realistic as well. The 26th of July Movement had to liberate Cuba *before* Cuba could become the internationalist contributor it is today. We know that the greatest contribution to internationalism (world revolution) is the primary struggle of self-determination. Of national liberation.

> We all know that the "United States" is an oppressor nation; that is, a nation that oppresses other nations. This is a characteristic that the u.s. shares with other imperialist powers. What is specific, in particular about the u.s. oppressor nation is that it is an illegitimate nation.
>
> What pretends to be one continental nation stretching from the Atlantic to the Pacific is really a euro-amerikan

settler empire, built on colonially oppressed nations and peoples whose very existence has been forcibly submerged. But the colonial crime, the criminals, the victims and the stolen lands and labor still exist. The many Indian nations, the New Afrikan nation in the South, Puerto Rico, the Northern half of Mexico, Asian Hawaii—all are now considered the lands of the euro-amerikan settlers. The true citizens of this u.s. empire are the European invaders and their descendants. So that the "United States" is in reality not one, but many nations (oppressor and oppressed). We see the recognition of amerika as a "prisonhouse of nations" as the beginning—no more, no less—of the differences between revisionist and communist politics here. We hold that once this outward shell of integration into a single, white dominated "U.S.A." is cracked open—to reveal the colonial oppression and anti-colonial struggle within— then the correct path to a communist understanding of the u.s. empire is begun.*

---

* Tani and Sera, pp. 9–10.

From Self-Doubt to Denial

The colonial mentality is insidious insofar as it blinds its victims with a dual sense of self-inadequacy. On the one hand, making the target people feel and believe that they in fact have no means by which to stand up, shake off and destroy the malady of apprehension and, on the other, that only the colonizing culture, its people included, have the answers, ability and means to solve any and all problems.

The colonial mentality is the 2.0 version of what We used to call the "slave mentality." It's a new and improved means of control, distraction and self-destruction. Wilson Goode, mayor of Philly, who greenlighted the bombing of the MOVE home, on May 13, 1985—2.0 version. Clarence Thomas, one of the u.s. conservative supremes—2.0. Rock Bottom, presidential front man for the u.s. ruling class—2.0. But these are the obvious ones, too easy to point out and light up. What of those who are so thoroughly imbued by a sense of self-inadequacy that they'd campaign for us to integrate our struggle—the only thing that We *have* maintained control over—into the so-called "workers movement" because they say this "... Is a step towards the total liberation of humanity and the whole world becoming one people"? Can't you just hear Louis Armstrong coonin' with that toothy grin, "What a Wonderful World"?

"Moreover," says the NABPP, "any such struggle [for National Territory] would almost certainly degenerate into an imperialist-sponsored race war, similar to what went down in Kosovo." (Cut the Louis Armstrong and queue the DMX—"Who We Be")

This is where basic logic, let alone political (revolutionary) consciousness, begins to fly completely apart from its center. What the NABPP is miserably failing to realize is that *colonialism is* an "imperialist-sponsored race war"! *Now*. It was one when the euros invaded Afrika, South Amerika, Asia and North Amerika. You think not? Ask the remnants of genocided peoples.

We use the words *nation* and *nationalities* to differentiate peoples and cultures, because We know that there really is no "plurality of races" on the planet. However, this usage of *words* doesn't necessarily alter—in fact, cannot alter—the fact that 13% of this planet are people of European descent and the other 87% are peoples from Afrika, South Amerika, North Amerika and Asia—or those considered of "color." Yet, the minority—who just "happens to be" from Europe—control the globe to their benefit and our demise.

Oh, there's a "race war" going on alright, but the colonial mentality has blinded some people behind a curtain of semantics which prevent the obvious conclusions from being drawn. Either that or...

Here's the thing: it has been *us*, the oppressed, who have prevented our total annihilation by waging national liberation struggles to repel pig aggression. The "imperialist-sponsored

Demonstration at New York City Hall, September 1978. (photo: Black Star)

race war" of *colonialism* (and neo-colonialjsm) has the NABPP so dazed and confused that they cannot recognize it for what it is. So, they project it instead into the future, as if it will "almost certainly" happen *if* We struggle for National Liberation. That's a manifestation, a symptom, of the colonial mentality. "Ooh, Momma, there go that man again!"

We found it curious that they'd project the "almost" certain "imperialist-sponsored race war" into the *future*, when Christopher Columbus, sponsored by King Ferdinand and Queen Isabella of Spain (certainly imperialists), landed in the Caribbean in 1492. Cortes, de Gama, Pizzaro, Magellan, Custer, Pershing, Westmoreland, Schwarzkopf, etc.—imperialists have *always* sponsored colonialist exploits. Trayvon Martin, Oscar Grant, Devin Brown, Lovelle Mixon, MLK, and countless other murders of our nationals can easily attest to the state of our existence, *now*. And We have social development, not to mention gaping holes in our cultures, to prove the past.

What We do know is that all this will continue if We do nothing. Or if We stand around nicely waiting for the very people, the 13% who benefit from our oppression, to unite with us in order to get free! We question with all seriousness the logic in this. We trust We are not alone.

Now, the same forces the NABPP attempts to threaten us with—those who the imperialists will "sponsor"—the NABPP says We should unite with because they "...are committed to supporting Black (sic) Liberation because it serves the cause of liberating all of humanity from imperialism and exploitation..." (queue the Benny Hill theme song). Where is self-determination in all of this? New Afrika is a working-class nation—with nothing to lose. Why not go deeper into *our own* nation for "support" in "liberating all of humanity"? When did the settlers get so "committed to supporting Black Liberation"?

The greatest "support" the settlers who are "committed" can offer the New Afrikan Independence Movement is to organize *their* nationals and start taking the fight to *their* bourgeoisie. That's *their* responsibility. Not uniting with us, or any other national liberation struggle. They have to build their own and handle their business. We'll run alliances when necessary, but their obligation is to not be "Good Americans"—not be like the Germans who were "Good Germans" during the Nazi era, just going right along with their government's genocidal programs because they were beneficial to them.

While We appreciate revolutionary solidarity, We first of all question any people as to what they are doing to tear down *their* ruling class and its machine? That's the criterion for solidarity. And why is that, you ask? Because:

> In a settler empire, one that is both a "prisonhouse" of
> Third World nations and peoples as well as the No. 1 im-
> perialist power, for young revolutionaries to be <u>uncertain</u>
> about proletarian internationalism inescapably means be-
> ing in practice uncertain about <u>parasitism</u>, uncertain about
> <u>solidarity</u>, and so on.* (our emphasis)

And being "uncertain" means being dead or captured. Radical integration and a blind, god-like allegiance to "super white folks" who are the only ones capable of helping us get free—if they don't, as the NABPP threatens, kill us all, in a "race war"—while literally having no faith in ourselves is, again, a symptom of colonial war mental disorder (colonial mentality). The only substantial treatment and cure for this is a deeper submersion of oneself into revolutionary consciousness through class suicide and struggle. Anything short of this will only perpetuate the malady.

---

* Tani and Sera, p. 141.

Some people talk about a "nation" but don't really wanna be one (independent), as evidenced by their efforts to crawl back on the plantation. How can We tell? You can identify those trying to crawl onto the plantation by the way they identify themselves, i.e., "blacks," "Afro-Amerikans," "Afrikan-Amerikans," "ethnic group," "minority nationality," "national minority," "underclass"—anything and everything except New Afrikans, an oppressed nation. Amerikkka is the plantation, and continuing to identify yourself within the amerikkkan context is evidence of the colonial ("slave") mentality. Ain't no two ways about it.

The NABPP says:

That We New Afrikans are now a predominantly proletarian nation and one without a National Territory—is an advantage to the cause…

Wrong again. New Afrikans have always been a proletarian nation. So much so in fact, that from 1619 to at least 1865, there was no unemployment in New Afrika—no woman, child nor man was exempt. (Imagine that.) It was called "slavery." And while the NABPP says We are "without a National Territory," the NAIM designated Louisiana, Mississippi, Alabama, Georgia and South Carolina as the National Territory as early as 1968:

On March 28, 1971, 150 New Afrikans held a "Nation Time" ceremony, consecrating 20 acres of newly-purchased land just west of Jackson, Mississippi. The land was designated as the future capital of the nation, named El Malik after Malcolm X (El Hajj Malik Shabazz). Fifteen new citizens took the "Nation Oath." President Imari Obadele

---

* Atiba Shanna, "Notes on Cadre Policy and Development," p. 10.

> *officiated at a New Afrikan wedding ceremony. Uniformed*
> *men and women of the Black Legion, the regular military*
> *of the Provisional Government of the Republic of New*
> *Afrika, patrolled the perimeter with rifles. Educational*
> *workshops, a meeting of the PG-RNA's People's Center*
> *Council, and other ceremonies filled the day.*[*]

So, again, as Yaki pointed out, for us there's never been a "question"—"only a task, a goal." The NABPP says that in 1978 our struggle for land was "revived" by the production of Harry Haywood's BBT. And yet in Black August of 1977, the New Afrikan Prisoners Organization wrote:

> *This piece was purposely concentrated on defining the 13th,*
> *14th, and 15th Amendments as instruments of national*
> *oppression because We believe that this is not only the*
> *most correct conception; but also because We believe this*
> *will contribute to raising the level of national conscious-*
> *ness among New Afrikan people and consequently to*
> *successful revolutionary nationalist war—a war for the*
> *independence of New Afrikan people, <u>a war to regain the</u>*
> *<u>National Territory</u>; a war which will lead to the establish-*
> *ment of sovereignty for New Afrika and its socialist de-*
> *velopment.*[†] *(our emphasis)*

We repeat: this is from 1977. Our eyes have never left the prize. So, We have a National Territory, it's just in the radical integrationist politics of the NABPP to first disagree that this is so, then to attempt to distort this reality and, failing that, to use

---

[*] Tani and Sera, p. 217.
[†] *Notes from a New Afrikan P.O.W. Journal, Book Two*, Spear and Shield Publications, 8-31-77.

deception through omission. Why, you may ask, would they do that? Well, according to them, New Afrikans' being

> ... *without a National Territory is an <u>advantage</u> to the <u>cause</u> of building a multi-ethnic, multi-racial socialist amerika. (our emphasis)*

And there it is—radical (reformist) integration. It is in their interests to disagree, distort and omit the facts in this regard. Which is why We believe that this piece on the so-called "national question"—while titled "Black Liberation in the 21st Century"— actually contributes little, if anything, towards "A Revolutionary Reassessment of Black Nationalism." It wasn't meant to do any such thing. It was designed to propagate radical (reformist) integration. We in the NAIM were simply a handy target.

If radical integration is their thing—well, that's their thing. They could very well have put forth their line without dragging us into it. If that's your bag, push it. We'll push ours. Ultimately, the masses will decide which line best suits their aspirations. But the NABPP has to come out with an attack on our line in their headlong rush in search of some imaginary "multi-ethnic, multi-racial" mass to lead. But wait, hmmm... *where* have We heard this before? (digging in the crates) Oh yeah, here it is:

> *When the U.S. Empire vamped on the BPP and they were, despite their intentions, unable to defend themselves, the Party strategy had failed. A new strategy was adopted. The Oakland BPP leadership turned to their natural ally, the euro-amerikan petty bourgeoisie. The Party leadership didn't turn to the New Afrikan proletariat because they neither knew how to organize the Nation nor did they really trust their own people. Their neo-colonial class unity with the white petty bourgeoisie came to the front in the*

> *crisis. This was justified as some kind of internationalism,*
> *of supposedly winning needed "allies" to the liberation*
> *movement.*[*]

But wait, there's more:

> *The Oakland leadership became committed to uniting with*
> *the settler petty bourgeoisie, if necessary (and it was)*
> *against their own national movement and against their*
> *former comrades.*[†]

The NABPP does another sleight of hand deception-by-omission when it speaks about Chairman Fred Hampton, of the Chicago chapter of the BPP, attempting to pass off his Rainbow Coalition as a paradigm for radical integration because there was an alliance with Mexicanos, Puerto Ricans, amerikans and New Afrikans. Here's what the NABPP conveniently failed to mention: the Brown Berets were a Chicano Nationalist Organization struggling to free their nation of Aztlán (Northern Mexico: California, Arizona, New Mexico, Texas and Nevada); the Young Lords Organization were Puerto Rican Independentistas struggling for the independence of their homeland. The New Afrikans in the Party at that time were still functioning under the Party's first line of New Afrikan nationalism. The settlers were struggling for a socialist amerika. So, it was an alliance of forces struggling for the national liberation of their respective productive forces—not to get together and sing Kumbaya. In the '70s things broke down, but when Chairman Fred was still alive, and in 1968–'69, this was the deal.

---

[*] Tani and Sera, p. 194.
[†] Ibid., p. 195.

No Need for a Nation State?

In a disturbingly blind-eyed distraction, the NABPP says:

> ... *Without need of pursuing a struggle to achieve a New Afrikan Nation State, We have achieved the historical results of bourgeois democracy at least as far as transforming ourselves from a peasant to a predominately proletarian national grouping through the "Great Migration."*

What? Again, We can't make this stuff up folks. We've always felt a need to pursue a New Afrikan Nation State. The struggle, on our side of the line, has always been about Freedom (Land), Independence (self-determination) and Socialism. In the New Afrikan Creed We find the following:

> *3. i believe in the community as more important than the individual.*

> *4. i believe in constant struggle for freedom, to end oppression and build a better world. i believe in collective struggle, in fashioning victory in concert with my brothers and sisters.*

> *5. i believe that the fundamental reason our oppression continues is that We as a people, lack the power to control our lives.*

> *6. i believe that the fundamental way to gain that power, and end oppression, is to build a sovereign Black nation.*

We have continuously pursued the need for a Nation State. The fact that We erected a Provisional Government, in 1968, should be testament enough. The fact of the matter is, there has always been, as in all things, a two line struggle in our nation. There has been a struggle to get out, free and independent of the empire, and another to get in to reform and wield the power of empire. That now We're faced with radical integrationism, in drag as some crackpot theory called "intercommunalism," doesn't change the twin essence of the two line struggle. This is nothing new.

The NABPP goes on to say:

> ... *We have achieved the historical results of bourgeois democracy.*

We have? Now, wait, is it bourgeois democracy or neo-colonialism? See, here's the very real difference in ideology. It is, as Comrad Yaki would say, "the contradiction surfacing and sharpening." If We are a part of a "multi-ethnic, multi-racial" "national grouping" (as the NABPP says) then yes, "We have achieved bourgeois democracy." That is, after all, what "multi-ethnics" get— you know, like the settler-garrison/citizens-of-empire, who came from Europe, or perhaps Oprah, Jordan, Rock Bottom and Wilson Goode. They get and can enjoy "bourgeois democracy"—that's the velvet glove. The masses of the oppressed nations, the internal colonies (New Afrika, Puerto Rico, Aztlán and Indigenous), well, We get the ol' iron fist of neo-colonialism, casino-freedom, common-wealth hegemony, barrio blues and ghetto prisons. But, of course, since We've had such success in "transforming ourselves from a peasant to a predominantly proletarian national grouping"... it's what? Better now? No, it's "an advantage to the cause of building a multi-ethnic multi-racial socialist amerika." What a wonderful thing, huh? Hey, here's a novel idea, why not all the internal colonies struggle to free the(ir) land and We break the empire apart like what happened with the USSR-empire? Too complicated, huh? "Comrade" Stalin wouldn't approve?

Internationalism, Real or False?

In a stunning turn in their already wildly contradictory and in-consistent phraseology, the NABPP says:

> *There are many white comrades (communists, socialists, anarchists and progressives) who are committed to sup-porting Black Liberation because it serves the cause of liberating all of humanity from imperialism and because it strengthens the workers' movement.*

If these comrades are communists, socialists, anarchists or pro-gressives (whatever that is?) why would the NABPP feel a need to tell us their complexion? What would their so-called "color" have to do with anything if they were comrades? See how subtle that is—it's like a magic spell—"white comrades." That's that colonial mentality bleeding thru—that which has the NABPP hypnotized is what they attempt to hypnotize others with. It's a subtle whimper that squeaks: "We can make it now, the domi-nant culture—mighty whitey—is with us." And the Comrades in the NABPP may not even be altogether aware of this, but it is what it is. If there are communists, socialists, anarchists and progressives (what the hell is that?) who are amerikans, canadi-ans or French, English, Irish or German who are "committed to supporting 'Black Liberation,'" then the best way to do that is to organize your people and attack your ruling class. If you got any extra weapons, slide them our way, please.

But having to explain that these comrades are "white" says more about the NABPP than it does about those who want to help. Isn't it strange how this so-called position on the national ques-tion is called "A Revolutionary Reassessment of Black Nationalism" but the NABPP is the main one clinging to terms which reinforce the false construct of "race"—like "white" and "black"? And, what about the fact that when it's *National* Liberation it's unbelieving scare quotes on *Liberation*—but when it's about "white comrades who are committed to supporting *Black* Liberation" the unbelieving scare quotes miraculously vanish? All of a sudden Black Liberation is something to "support"?

What's also puzzling—the NABPP says the "white comrades" are committed to supporting "Black Liberation because it serves the cause of liberating all of humanity from imperialism and because it strengthens the workers' movement." We'd hate to come off as knit-picking, but *what* workers' movement? Does anyone else *smell* that?

Check this out:

> ... *There are many individual euro-amerikan workers but they do not make up a genuine proletariat. That is, settler workers are a non-exploited labor aristocracy, with a privileged lifestyle far, far above the levels of the world proletariat. They might be called a pseudo-proletariat, in that individual settlers do work in factories and mines, but as a group they do not perform the role of a proletariat. Settler workers neither support their society by their labor, nor is their exploitation the source of the surplus value (or profit) that sustains the u.s. bourgeoisie. The life-giving role of the proletariat in the u.s. empire is relegated to the proletarians of the oppressed nations, which is why "nations become almost as classes" under imperialism. The shrinking number of settler workers actually live as part of the lower petty bourgeoisie and have no separate political existence. Classes in the U.S. Empire themselves reflect the primary contradiction between imperialism and the oppressed nations.*[*]

---

[*] Ibid., p. 5.

No wonder the NABPP says the settlers will support us—"it strengthens the workers' movement," and furthermore, "The cause of uniting the Black liberation struggle with the proletarian class struggle is a step towards the total liberation of humanity and the whole world becoming one people."

Now it's the "Black Liberation *struggle*"? What would that struggle be for? Pursuing a Nation State maybe? Land? So, We are to forego our struggle for Land, Independence and Socialism, to unite with who? "The proletarian class"—We *are* the proletarians!! And how 'bout that "liberation of humanity and the whole world becoming one people"? White folks sure are powerfully magic, ain't they, sah? Yes, sah, mighty powerful! (hat in hand, staring off into the distance, mouth agape like an idiot)

This is radical—and at times comical—integration—it's more of what We've always had. Nothing new here. No groundbreaking great leap forward.

We'll close out with a quote by a Comrad in hopes of some receptive ear feeling the vibrations of revolutionary nationalism. Dig this:

> *The key to the destruction of the empire lies stirring within it. Not outside. The head and heart, brain and nerves—all vital organs essential to the perpetuation of life—are all inside, not outside.*

> *What will be critical, what is fundamental and essential for the initiation of a socialist world, is the eventual liberation of New Afrika, and other oppressed nations inside the belly of the amerikkan empire.*

> *Not 1917 or 1978 Russia. Not 1949 or 1978 China. Not Cuba, Vietnam, Mozambique, Angola, Zimbabwe or Azania; not Brazil, Chile—neither of these nor any*

other place outside the belly of the empire will alone or together truly free the world from the grips and threats of amerikkkan capitalism, imperialism, colonialism or neo-colonialism.

They may help. They will cause change of conditions and create a climate offering greater potential, higher probabilities and increased chances of success... but not until the head and heart, brain and nerves—until the vital organs are destroyed, the empire will simply re-adjust. Re-form. Make new alliances. It will change form, but it will live— so long as New Afrika is subjugated. So long as Puerto Rico is a colony or neo-colony. So long as Native nations don't have sovereignty over their lands and lives.*

The struggle is for Land, Independence and Socialism. We'll see you in the whirlwind!

---

* Ibid.

On Correct Terminology and Spellings
En Route to Conscious Development and Socialist Revolution

There has been some dialogue generated recently that has come to focus on the way the New Afrikan Independence Movement (NAIM) uses certain spellings, particular words, phrases and slogans to distinguish, apply energy, weight and clarity to the ongoing and ever-increasing need for sharper, more critical, words of power to describe the socio-economic phenomena of national oppression.

What We'd like to do here is go through a few of these in use now which are generally accepted as a standard for cadres of NAIM, but may not be so obvious to others. And, too, the thing We'd like to do is open up a deeper line of dialogue, in this regard, in hopes of developing a unified theory of comprehensive terminology to enhance the depth, breadth and momentum of revolutionary consciousness as We build for People's War (Vita Wa Watu).*

In our struggle to regain independence as a self-determining people, with dignity and pride, We overstand that We must have a national identity, a name. One that is neither given by our oppressors nor predicated on a racialist color. We must have

---

* *Vita Wa Watu*: Swahili meaning People's War.

Captured Afrikans being marched to the coast, from where they would be transported to St. Domingue, 1786.

a nationality, as a pre-requisite, if We are serious about forging the socio-economic constructs of a State by which to govern the nation(ality), i.e. the people/citizens. We necessarily begin at the beginning. We *know* We are descended from peoples forcefully removed from the West Coast of the Afrikan continent. We *know* We haven't fallen from the sky. We also have sure knowledge of the reasons We were brought here. But, Afrika is a *continent* of many people, and not a homogenous nation; it isn't now, nor was it when the predators and destroyers came and probably hadn't been since the early, early days of life.

On the continent there are nations and nationalities. There are various languages, cultures, politics, religions and customs. So, We know what when the predators and destroyers came they found many different people. We know they made deals with some to work in concert against others. It was a socio-economic arrangement—a class alliance. Supply and demand. We often heard growing up, by amerikans, who wished to distance

Captured Afrikans traversing the Middle Passage, 1849.

themselves from colonialism, that "your own people sold you into slavery." Well, this is not altogether true, since essentially We'd never really all been *one people*—certainly not by the time the predators came—and even among those of the same nation, there were class divisions and other contradictions. What We all were, however, was dark. Darker in complexion by far than the Europeans or the Arabs who came assailing us. And thus it was this apparent "difference" that *they* seized upon to make us "one people"—*black* people first, then Afrikan, as a whole. Much like capitalism is now making all Spanish-speaking people into Latinos and/or Hispanics. Or how colonialism made all Indigenous people into "Indians." But underneath this generalization were *nationalities* and nations. We knew this, certainly. For had you asked a captured woman who she was, say in 1580, she would not have said "i'm black," nor would she have said "i'm Afrikan." She'd have said "i am Akan" or "i am Fante," or Hausa, Ibo, Fulani, Ewe, Yoruba, etc.

It was these various peoples, hailing from numerous nations and nationalities, that were brought together under colonialism and transported to the so-called "New World" to be utilized as a proletariat for the new European nations being built on stolen and occupied lands. By dint of brutal transport and collusion We were brought together under conditions less than human and barely tolerable. By our own internal dynamics and self-motion We essentially combined in these conditions to become a *new* people. No longer Ibo, Fulani, Ewe, Fante or Yoruba—but Afrikan still. Our cultures weren't so much destroyed as they were *transformed*. We survived and remade ourselves on the residue of self-consciousness/self-motion. In a 100% hostile environment.

Of this We have sure knowledge. That from Los Angeles to New York and all areas in between, New Afrikans share the *same* culture our ancestors forged in the cauldron of old colonialism. You know how the bourgeois media likes to parrot Boy Bush by saying "9-11 changed everything?" Well, in actuality, colonialism is really what *changed* everything—really. For just as We became a New Afrikan nation in North America, Indigenous nations were being decimated and a *new* European Nation-State called amerika was coming into existence.

This is how nations are really formed—how nationalities come to be. They don't mysteriously fall, ready-made, from the sky. It is human nature to bring into existence new unities (nations/nationalities) based on need or greed. So, while We may have come here as Fulani, Ewe, Ibo, etc., this is not who We are today. While simultaneously the Fulani, Ewe and Ibo people *still* exist in Afrika. The reality is, however, *We* can't go back to the past. We'd be insincere running around Oakland or Brooklyn talking about "i'm Yoruba," "i'm Hausa"—cause We are not. Not anymore. We have our own customs now. Our own culture, too. And even though We are saddled with the colonial language, We have our own ways of using it to suit our needs. We now have our own set of contradictions that are unique to our particular social development *here*. And yet We are still Afrikan. Though We've come to overstand that being Afrikan wasn't enough to describe our particular experience and social development *here*. Nor was it sufficient to point us in the direction of where We need to go—that is, when and where We enter, again, onto the world stage of nations.

We keep emphasizing nationality and nation here because if you think about it—meditate on it—We can't enter the world community of nations as "minorities," as "blacks" or as "African Americans." That would be absurd. Why, it would be akin to us going out reppin' amerika, the u.s. government, capitalism/imperialism and all that this entails. We'd be bourgeois amerikan nationalists. And don't fool yourself, you'd *still* be a nationalist—you'd just be a bourgeois nationalist. That is, you'd be a representative of the new unity that amerika is under its ruling class—with all that this entails. So, We emphasize nationality and nation in order to bring the reality out that it is a choice one has, whether to side with the colonizer or to struggle with the oppressed, which is essentially to struggle *against* oppression. *Against* u.s. capitalism/imperialism. *Against* being colonized and prevented from being yourself.

We have chosen New Afrikan as our nationality because it adequately defines our experience. It brings the reality of our transformation and new unity right down to where it needs to be. It also affords us an identity of our own, out and away from that given to us by our oppressors:

> *"New Afrikan" reflects our identity as a nation and a people—a nation and a people desiring self-determination. New Afrikans have been called "colored Americans," "American Negroes," "Black Americans" and "Afro-Americans."*

> *"New Afrikan" reflects our purpose as We desire freedom,*
> *self-determination and independence. By stating We are*
> *New Afrikans, We clarify We want to be independent*
> *from the amerikkkan empire. We want Land and National*
> *Liberation. We no longer want the ruling class of the*
> *amerikkkan empire to determine our political, economic,*
> *socio-cultural affairs.* *

We also have the New Afrikan Declaration of Independence, the New Afrikan Creed and the Code of Umoja written and ratified in 1968, with a subsequent review completed by the People's Center Council, on November 3, 2007. These lofty documents point to the reality of our national existence.

Comrad-Brotha Owusu Yaki Yakubu pointed out on many occasions that: "The Nation exists both in potentiality and actuality—it's just not free."

The reason We need to get past the usage of labels like "black" and "African American" is because they only serve to distort our reality. These labels confuse and misdirect the colonialism of the u.s. into an "Everything's Better Now" fog of narcolepsy.

Another way this is done is by calling our experience here, from 1619 to 1865, mere "slavery." When, of course, it was much worse, more complex and binding that any slavery ever could be. Saying our condition was mere "slavery" is an easy way out; it is to say "slavery was abolished in 1865 with the ratification of the 13th amendment." Which then leads to the 14th amendment to make New Afrikans "citizens"—thereby violating our human right to self-determination, but also liquidating the reality of our nation by incorporating us into the empire as "minority

---

* From the New Afrikan Peoples Organization's newspaper *By Any Means Necessary.*

citizens"—as "negroes," "blacks," "colored," "African Americans"—
as those who cannot govern themselves, whose productive forces
are harnessed by the empire for its own interests. What they
never want us to overstand is that We *are* a nation *inside* the belly
of the beast. No, this reality must always be distorted, disguised,
laughed at, slapped away or crushed.

In a way, our finding and usage of the correct terminology
to facilitate an overstanding of colonialism, comes as a means to
combat the enemy's mass distortions of our reality. Yes, this is
true. You see, the conscious instinctively go East when the enemy
insists the right way is West. We refuse to move along its path;
We stop, stand our ground and struggle *against* the stream because We know our truths. Our interests stand in stark contrast
to the enemy's. So, We dig in search of the tools We'll need to end
its life. And isn't that what it does too, in order to oppress us?
We're in the *same* war—We're just on different sides.

Just as We are not black, negro, or African American, our
condition was not "slavery." Which is not to say our condition
didn't have the outward appearance of slavery. Nor are We trying to take anything away from the awful conditions which our
ancestors endured. We are saying that "slavery," like those "minority" labels, is a distortion of the facts. In order to fully ap-
prehend reality, We cannot use the deliberately faulty tools given
us by our enemies. When using *their* analyses of our condition
We'll get *their* results—which favor *their* distortions and continuing oppression of us as "minorities" or "disenfranchised second
class citizens." How can anyone be *dis*-enfranchised when they've
never been *en*-franchised?! Oh, but We *were en*-franchised, as a
colony—like, individuals can own a McDonald's, but have to go to
Ronald McDonald College in order to learn how to run the business in accordance with the overall standards of established order
of the corporation. The same food, same colors, same uniforms,

same culture of the corporation permeates *all*. But now check this out: wouldn't *real dis*-enfranchisement mean to *leave* the corporate orbit—to get free of it? That's what We should be struggling for: disenfranchisement, no? We're looking for correct terminology. For ways out. We're not struggling to be *en*-franchised. But We want true disfranchisement and not some fake, paperweight, bantustan, flag freedom.

We've been told that being born here makes us amerikans. We reject that foolishness. We are more apt to ride with the sobering words of Malcolm X: "Being born here doesn't make you an amerikan. Why, that's like saying if a cat has kittens in the oven that makes them biscuits." You might want to read that one again.

Having made the points We have We'll move this along. Though not without a quote from Comrad-Brotha Owusu Yaki Yakubu:

> The "native," the "negro," the "colored," the "black," and the "African-American," have no identity apart from that given them by the colonizer—that is, not unless they resist colonialism, which entails: 1) their maintenance of an identity that is separate and distinct from that of the colonized and from that given them by the colonizer; 2) they begin to develop a new identity, through the process of "decolonization"—though having remained separate and distinct, colonized people aren't who they were prior to colonization, and they can't return to the past. Colonization has arrested their independent development, distorted who they are, and now they must become (a) new people during the process by which they regain their independence.[*]

---

[*] Sayles, p. 168.

The _new_ people need a new, more critical (and radical) set of words, of terminology, to bring the "arrested development" of our independence into sharper focus. A focus so clear as to give us the ability to read the earth signs and guideposts towards national independence and socialism. The struggle, lest We forget, is not just *against* capitalism/imperialism, but also *for* socialism. We are not trying to get a seat at the table or an office in the Whitest House. That's called reform. That's called collusion, collaboration and neo-colonialism. That's not our bag. We suggest strongly that all New Afrikans seek to obtain, study and meditate on the following documents:

→ the New Afrikan Declaration of Independence
→ the New Afrikan Creed
→ the Code of Umoja (Republic of New Afrika's National Constitution)

These, of course, are the general laws, ethics and obligations of New Afrikan nationals. Individual collectives and orgs in the NAIM will necessarily have their own particular bylaws, codes of ethics and points of authority to frame their practice vis-à-vis the masses and other collectives orgs. Nonetheless, We all function under the general/objective laws established by the Provisional Government.

What tends to bother us is when comrades from other movements and nationalities, who've struggled with us in various capabilities, do interviews or in their writings, refer to us as "African Americans" or "blacks." And We're not talking about the average comrades on the street who have no real clue about our ideology—no, We mean comrades who, in some instances, were captured with some of our nationals. It's not cool to do that. We feel that if you want to be "politically correct," then side with the revolutionaries and not with the distortionists. We are New Afrikans. In 1968, over 500 New Afrikan nationalists signed the New Afrikan Declaration of Independence and named our nation the Republic of New Afrika. We feel when comrades do that they are going along with our oppression. At least some form of it. They are conscious, they know better. And, too, We have to step up our ideological struggle to deepen the correct usage of our national identity. Even in low tides We must stand firm and push forward.

Some Terms/Spellings

1.   We, as a rule, capitalize the "W" in We to emphasize the collective/mass importance of the people. We overstand that capitalism and the degenerate culture that inherently flows from it, incites, facilitates and rewards rank individualism. It fosters the "me, me, me," "look out for Number 1" and "i am more important than all of you" mentality.

In amerika, for example, one individual can own 10 (or 100) supermarkets and feel or have no obligation to feed *one* hungry person. In fact, owners have had poor people prosecuted to the full extent of bourgeois law, for taking food; or homeless people for panhandling on his/her premises. Individualism, gluttonous consumerism and naked greed are the inherent hallmarks of capitalism. We necessarily reflect this and thus capitalize our W's and simultaneously de-capitalize (cut the head off) the "i" when it's used in a *"normative case singular of the first person pronoun"* or as *"the word used by a speaker or written in mentioning [herself]/himself."* We feel that doing so not only keeps us focused but is also instructive to our readers. Some Comrads have decapped

---

* *Webster's Integrated Dictionary and Thesaurus.*

their whole names to further illustrate their submergence in the people.

2.   We spell Afrika with a "K" as opposed to a "C" because as Comrad-Brotha Sundiata pointed out:

> ... the New Afrikan Independent Movement spells Afrikan with a "K" as an indicator of our cultural identification with the Afrikan continent and because Afrikan linguists originally used "K" to indicate the "C" sound in the English language.*

We also use the "K" in our national identity to illustrate our break with and necessary distinction from our colonizers. The "K" represents resistance, rebellion and our need for critical distance from the normative constraints of colonialism.

3.   We, by and large, de-cap the "A" in amerika for several reasons. Principal among these is the fact that the colonial State is an illegal settler government/empire fastened, by dint of genocide and colonialism (colonial violence), onto the backs of Indigenous nations/land and other internal colonies. We overstand the u.s. as a virtual—nay, as an *actual*—prisonhouse of nations which are culturally and economically held in check by a complicit garrison population of citizens who believe in amerikan exceptionalism, manifest destiny and the inherent inferiority of everyone but themselves. These amerikans are fortified ideological shocktroops holding the genocidal quilt of u.s. imperialism together with boundless acts of blind-ass patriotism and loyalty. We reject that and refuse to give this (or any) empire any acknowledgment as a place of peace, liberty and democracy. Amerika is not

---

* Sundiata Acoli, *Updated History of the New Afrikan Prison Struggle*.

so much a place, deserving a capital letter at its helm, as it is an *experience*, like a wild and horrifying ride at an amusement park—only this ride is more lethal, a thousand times more harmful and totally mind-warping. "The ride of a lifetime," where whole nations are strapped in for the violent twists and turns of empire. The more We try to get off, the faster it goes, the higher it climbs, the deeper it plunges—Welcome to the Terror Dome!!! We are not in the habit of giving respect to those who don't respect us. Decap the "A."

4.   We use a "K" (or three Ks) in amerikkka—as We do in the word "kkkountry" when referring to amerika and its capitalist allies—to emphasize our awareness that it is the prototype, the archetype, of the Ku Klux Klan. Its overall reactionary, racialist, and theological schematic is Klannish! And just because the State employs functionaries from its colonies means nothing. The ruling class is a seething cauldron of alabaster menace. Sitting, as it does, atop the planet, in a predator's pose, ready to pounce on the next crime to make a profit; the pathological bourgeoisie is the brain trust of every two-bit supremacist on the planet. The

Klan foremost among them. We think it was the Amazon Butch Lee who said, "amerika is what nazi germany wanted to be." We agree and would go on to add that the ruling class is who the Klan aspires to be like and keep in power. So, We necessarily associate the two in our writings because it keeps us focused on the fundamental contradiction in our way. Would you want to integrate into a Klan society?

5.   Some of us younger comrades will use a capital "O" on *our* or "U" on *us* when referring to New Afrikan people. This is but a particular style used by those of us in the trenches doing ideological combat on a daily basis. It is a good concept to promote the unitarian ideal, however, it often brutalizes the written text by detracting from the smooth flow of a sentence. Not to mention being a virtual nightmare for some of our comrades who help in transcribing our work. And, too, We'll often use these caps this way to stand to the left of those who've come before us. However, all ideas are not of equal value and any theory which cannot stand up to objective reality is dead. While We don't think the concept dead, We do, however feel it's not practical. For as long as We wrap up the "W" and cut the head off of that big-ass "i" We'll be fine.

6.   As revolutionary nationalists We are, without question, antiracists. We work diligently to exclude all language (and practice) that promotes or perpetuates the false social construct of "race." We first of all get past this by overstanding who concocted this foolishness. Oh yeah... it was the *same* class of predators who constantly told us to go West—"It's the right way, the only way out." No bet. Trust and believe when they say go West—your surest path is in *any other* direction. Let's check in with the wise counsel of Comrad-Brotha Owusu Yaki Yakubu:

> "Racism" is used to justify and facilitate the exploitation of
> peoples, and it's based on the false belief that humanity
> is divided into a plurality of "races" that stand in relation
> to each other as "inferior" or "superior" based on physical
> and/or cultural differences. There are no "races"—only
> people(s) and groups of people(s), united and distinguished
> by common history (social development), habits, inter-
> ests, etc.—sometimes We call all of this "nationality" or
> ideology.
>
> To be "anti-racist" is, first of all, not to hold the false belief
> in an alleged plurality of "races"; to be "against racism" is
> to combat all beliefs and practices that facilitate the ex-
> ploitation of peoples, particularly when such explication is
> supported by the social construction of "race."*

What We do is stop calling ourselves "black." This goes along with
the false construct and perpetrates the erroneous belief. Not to
mention the colonial relationship of oppressed and oppressor. To
say "black" is to promote the "plurality of race"; the "black race,"
"white race," etc. People have *national* identities. We are not racists, so why promote racist beliefs? Now, We are not naïve, either.
While We know the science behind the division of humanity into
races is, without question, junk science and crackpot engineering, We also overstand that regular folks ain't got that memo.
The masses of all colonies inside the beast still function under
this guise. And so while *We* overstand it's not real, people are still
quite willing to kill and die for it. But We have to lead the way of
"de-colonizing," "dis-enfranchising" and de-programming them.
So, "race" is both false and to an extent "real."

Let's go over to the dictionary and see what it says about the

---

* Sayles, p. 157.

two words in question. We're using a 2006, *Webster's Integrated Dictionary and Thesaurus*:

> *Black: adj. of the darkest color, like coal or soot; having dark-colored skin and hair, especially Negro; without light; dirty; evil; wicked; sad, dismal; sullen...*

We could go on with the description, but it only gets worse. Let's flip over to the word "white" (same source) and see what We find:

> *White: adj. of the color of milk or pure salt; stainless; pure; bright; light-colored, as of caucasoid skin; color of anything white, innocent...*

Well, We know these are wholly inadequate terms to use in referring to people, any people. And We overstand, too, that "black" was sort of necessary in the 1960s to distinguish the revolutionaries from the neo-colonialist negroes. However, We also know that it was insufficient and should now be put to rest. Along with "white." We are more concerned with one's politics than We are with anyone's complexion. We unite with those whose practice and sincerity bears them out to be worthy. We are birthed into this world with no control over our complexions (pigmentation)—our nationality and our politics, however, We can choose. That's the basis of the get down. The content of character, practice and the company one keeps are always the surest indicators of who's who.

In our writings, speaking and organizing, We make that *national* distinction between us and amerikans based not on "race"—"black" or "white"—as if We were all "Americans" with just different complexions, who suffer or prosper as a result of a few bad men/women in office. No, We clarify the reality based on oppressor and oppressed *nations*. On capitalism versus socialism. On national independence versus colonialism. As soon as We

fall into the trap of "race," We lose momentum—We stop pushing our line and start pushing the colonizers' line. We heighten
awareness by exposing the falsehoods. The contradictions are
plentiful and there is no shortage of angles for us to attack. The
fundamental contradiction is not "race," but national oppression,
with fat-ass u.s. imperialism sitting on our backs preventing us
from moving in our own national interests. The struggle is to destroy this overbearing bully, to get free and in the process rebuild
ourselves into productive people who are about world revolution
and socialism.

"Hands Off Angela Davis" N.Y.C. – 1970 © Luis C. Garza (all rights reserved)

7.   We are anti-patriarchal—which entails us being against *all*
forms of male supremacy and suppression of women. Women
hold up half the sky—and in most oppressed nations, it's more
like three quarters. This is especially true in New Afrika. We necessarily combat any and all forms of gender oppression. While
We'd like to say such oppression is a result of capitalist economics, that would unfortunately not be true; We believe and have
sure knowledge that men turned women and children into the

first oppressed populations on the planet, long before capitalism appeared on the scene. Patriarchy is a backwards, oppressive and exploitative form of social (and personal) relations that infects and warps the activity of otherwise progressive or potentially revolutionary women and young girls. So, what We do is be pro-actively corrective in not only our practice, but also in our writings and our speech.

Male-centered language runs rampant through most cultures as does practice. Have you ever stopped to ponder any of the words We think are "normal"—words like: *manpower, manhours, manhole, mankind,* etc.—and these are but a few of the more flagrant ones.

Think about organized religion too. What effect does it have on women and young girls, on boys and men for that matter, who feel an inherent sense of entitlement, due to its unflinching patriarchy? For in every one of the major religions god supposedly only picked men (in one, *his* son) to be prophets or saviors. The last person god spoke with or communicated to, or called upon to lead, was a man. One major religion takes the mother totally out of the equation making for only the father, the son and the "holy spirit." Some others offer "virgins" as rewards for martyrdom—owned and possessed even in paradise. The major organized religions are in fact good ol' boy networks that relegate women and children to near chattel status as submissives and victims of men. It is as if in order to get into "heaven," "paradise" or whatever land of pleasure and ease one believes in, women and children must have been good submissives and supporters, mere bit-players, to their husbands, brothers and fathers. Or loyal to their priest, imam or rabbi. Well, We reject that. We refuse to see women as inferiors, or objects and needing and having to have the guards, protection or sympathy of men in order to "get along" or to get to some far-off paradise. Fuck that!

We believe and have sure knowledge that women possess the very same potential as any man to change the world. Perhaps even more so. We know women can govern, guide, lead, fight, struggle, conspire, shoot, theorize and everything else any man can do—and have done so. And yet women have been so oppressed by men that they are very distrustful and suspicious and We say rightfully so. But We overstand that unity of purpose, of need and necessity grows out of steadfast practice and righteousness. Simultaneously, We overstand that women and children need and *must* have a military strategy of their own. Must always stand ready. We recognize this is true, because revolutions, too, can and have turned into good ol' boy networks. To be cautious is to be aware of all this. Be mindful of social relations that do harm to the unintended, to those We must unite with; to those who are the most oppressed. It is about being accountable and responsible. *That's* revolutionary!

What We do is change words like "mankind" to *humankind*. "History" to *social development*, or ourstory. Or to emphasize that it is a lie told by our colonizers, We'll spell it as *his-story* (as in male-centered and just "his" version).

Women in the collectives, orgs and movement will use *her-story*. Which is perfectly natural, really, given how much of the social development of women—especially Amazons—has been *man*handled, buried, distorted or lied about. We encourage women to do the damn thing! Right on! When We write We need to be mindful that the Nation ain't "he" or "him." Not made up of just males. Use the slash mark ("/") to always include both genders. And these are but the rudiments, mere seeds beneath the snow. We'll necessarily build on these as We grow and develop—and as women/Amazons push out front and exert themselves so their own reality is widely representative of the whole. Learn how they wish to be related to by them.

8. We are against homophobia. But deeper still, We are about combating heterosexism. See, homophobia—the irrational fear of someone because of their sexual orientation—is but one side of the equation. One can be "in fear" and use this to run away, or avoid the natural in order to make themselves feel better, but this will only give rise to homophobia's evil twin—heterosexism. Which is not just fear of, but oppression and exploitation of someone based on their sexual orientation. It points to a degenerate set of politics, for it always comes back to our politics. Our politics are revolutionary, naturally against oppression and yet here We are oppressing someone based on their natural self. If We kept our politics in command We'd know better. We'd do better.

We need to be clear and focused here cause people will try to get by on this. If We are going to be the message We bring then We have to stand firm on our politics. People, collectives and orgs will profess that they are not homophobic—have no fear of gays, lesbians, bisexuals or transgendered people—and yet go right on to practice staunch heterosexism by having not one post in their orgs held by gays, lesbians, bisexuals or transgender people. All those in any position of power are so-called "straight" people. To us, any org claiming to be revolutionary or representative of the people, that doesn't actively recruit, promote and cultivate gays, lesbians, bisexuals and transgender people/cadres, is not really pushing a revolutionary line for change and freedom—let alone socialism. They are perpetuating the backwardness of the bourgeoisie—hell, We can hardly say *that* anymore since even reactionaries have repealed their heterosexist policies.

We are concerned about a person's character, politics, practice and the company they keep. Not their complexion, gender or sexual orientation. The question is—and should always be—are they down for revolution? Are they with us or against us? Do they overstand that We are about armed struggle? We are not those to sit-in, love-in, cry-in or hold hands and sing "We shall overcome." That's not us. We are about armed struggle.

So, in our writings We don't just condemn homophobia— We also shine the light on heterosexism. On so-called "straight" domination of things as if being hetero is any indication of being always right or somehow real. Give us a break! What's going to guide us is revolutionary consciousness, informed by our political line. And the fact of the matter is if you're not ready to let consciousness guide you—truly, you're not ready for revolution, i.e. for complete change.

9. We recognize koncentration kamps ("prisons") in the u.s. as tools of colonial violence used to further arrest the development of national independence. Koncentration kamps, like the kourts, the bourgeois law and the political police are all tied into the matrix of imperialism. For settlers these places are *prisons*. For colonial subjects, citizens of the internal nations, these are koncentration kamps—intentional, political, containing and genocidal. In a monopoly capitalist society with a deeply entrenched ruling class, such as exists here in amerika, no facet of its system is beyond the pale of economic pressure and control. That is, *all* oppressive parts related to the whole are subject to the scrutiny of the ruling class. In other words, they serve the needs of the beast. Profit and disposal. Everything worthwhile is tied, in some way, to the profit motive/margin of monopoly capitalism. Koncentration kamps in this regard are major holdings for the bourgeoisie because they serve two purposes: they pen up potential "social dynamite," those most likely to resist and rebel and revolt. And then they also exploit this same legion as industrial laborers in the kamps. But deeper still, this system also gives jobs to settlers who work in those kamps as guards, managers, nurses,

doctors, counselors, etc. We spell koncentration kamps with a "K" for the same reasons We use the K's in *amerika*, *kourt* and *kountry*. It's all Klannish.

And so it is that We've come to the end of these notes. We hope to have brought some light and reason to some of the things We are about, that We struggle around and that We tend to bring to completion. We are under no illusions—have no thoughts of anything being easy or quick. We are committed for the duration, come what may. We shall enter with our heads up, backs straight, focused and conscious. We urge you to join the revolution and get down for the freedom you so richly deserve. We have nothing to lose but our chains.

Pathology of Patriarchy
A Search for Clues at the Scene of the Crime

The great divide between humans and animals provided a standard by which to judge other people, both at home and elsewhere. If the essence of humanity was defined as consisting of a specific quality or set of qualities, such as reason, intelligible language, religion, culture, or manners, it followed that anyone who did not fully possess those qualities was "subhuman." Those judged less than human were seen either as useful beasts to be curbed, domesticated, and kept docile, or as predators or vermin to be eliminated.*

What We are going to do here is direct your attention to the pathology of oppression, but not simply as you are used to reading about it. The obvious points of contention will inevitably be touched on as they relate, as attendant ills, to the subject at hand, however We will try to keep our focus—and your attention—trained on the issue in play! Please bear with us as We move along to connect the dots.

We want to talk about homophobia—the fear and oppression of gays, lesbians, bisexuals and transgender people. And We want to discuss this because as revolutionaries it is our duty to deal with all socio-economic and political phenomena that

---

* Charles Patterson, *Eternal Treblinka*.

engages our reality (past, present and future). The obligation of the revolutionary is to make the revolution. That is to change oneself, encourage the people to change and then change the current system that oppresses. Of course, it would be ideal if, in 2012, We didn't have to even deal with this matter. We wish that these issues had been resolved during the last high tide of consciousness. But sadly, that was not the case—and so here We are. No matter, the sooner begun, the sooner done, no? Right on!

We are learning as We go to recognize, overstand, isolate and deal with maladies as they arise, but have just begun to tie all these into the oppressive matrix of patriarchy as the origin of major isms that crush, kill, disrupt and destroy—as they oppress and exploit. It's unfortunate, but We're having to start from scratch every thirty or forty years because We lack a continuity of consciousness in our struggle against capitalist-imperialism. And while issues of sexism have been dealt with in large part by women, it's necessary to broaden the scope of the discussion of sexism to include homophobia and heterosexism. We are not in any way claiming to be experts on this issue. We are studying and struggling around the same things that most revolutionaries are— which is to say, We are looking for clues at the scene of the crime. Trying to connect the dots as they relate to individual, national and global oppression. We are, in essence, looking for ways to get free and stay free. Free, that is, from *all* forms of oppression.

Here's the thing: if people are being oppressed because of who they naturally are (and We know this to be true), which may not fit into a patriarchal gender box, then this is due to a "sex" (or gender) issue. So We feel this still covers sex-ism. In other words, that patriarchy (male dominated systems of oppression) create categories for people to fit into in order to exploit and oppress. Therefore, so-called genders then become classes. A class of men, the dominant—masculine, violent, god, father, king, president, boss, etc.—and a class of women, the dominated—feminine, passive, holy ghost, homemaker, whore, etc. Oppression by "sex" is the oldest form of oppression on the planet. Older than institutionalized theocracies like Judaism, Christianity and Islam. Theocratic regimes institutionalized male dominant systems of oppression thru laws, State bureaucracies and social relations. In fact, men deal with women and children as they did livestock.

> *Nowhere is patriarchy's iron fist as naked as in the oppression of animals, which serves as the model and training ground for all other forms of oppression.*[*]

Pathological Progression of Patriarchy

Why is it necessary to speak about patriarchy if We are discussing homophobia? And, why begin with the oppression of women and children if this is about oppression of gender outlaws? Well, what We have to do is a bit of excavation—some radical anthropology, if you will, because the fact of the matter is, We know that things don't fall from the sky or magically appear out of thin air. We are looking for connections, contradictions and from these We'll be rewarded with the truth of origins and the internal dynamics in the life process of the thing. The "thing" in this particular study is oppression as manifested thru the system of patriarchy—which We contend is the origin of a vast array of other forms of oppression. Which is precisely why We brought in the domestication of animals. We are learning that the same techniques used to domesticate animals were also used in the colonization of women and children and eventually every culture they encountered.

---

* Aviva Cantor, *The Club, the Yoke, and the Leash: What Can We Learn From the Way a Culture Treats Animals.* MS (August 1983).

Breeding, birth control, castration, segregation, exploitation and mass murder were methods learned first on animals and *then* on humans. And there was always a symbiotic relationship of know-how used between the two areas of domestication, including their mass killing for capitalist markets and the mass production of commodities, such as cars, in the development of capitalist industry:

> In his autobiography <u>My Life and Work</u> (1922) Henry Ford revealed that his inspiration for assembly-line production came from a visit he made as a young man to a Chicago slaughterhouse. "I believe that this was the first moving line ever installed," he wrote, "The idea [of the assembly line] came in a general way from the overhead trolley that the Chicago packers use in dressing beef."*

Capitalism came out of patriarchy, but We know that it is not exclusive to capitalism. It was a good ol' boy network *before* capitalism is recognized to have created modern classes. It was the same good ol' boy network under Soviet so-called "socialism" and it was a good ol' boy network in the civil rights movement and, to a large degree, in the Black Liberation Movement. Patriarchy positions itself above all as the reason, the answer and the solution—all to the detriment of women and children—but that's not all: patriarchy is a pervasive system of oppression that reaches far and wide into the minds and actions of all. It produces sexism, of course, but more insidiously it relies upon its victims to perpetuate and promote it. Again, there's no magic involved here. These things are *knowable*—and it follows that if We can identify, expose and challenge these things We can defeat them. Or, be

---

* Keith Thomas, *Man and the Natural World: A History of the Modern Sensibility.* (New York, Pantheon Books, 1983).

defeated. And, should We do nothing, this will most certainly insure that things get worse.

Oftentimes We miss the boat on overstanding the subtle ways We go about reinforcing patriarchal relationships in our daily lives, because domination is but one aspect of patriarchy. That's just the obvious aspect of it. You know, like when Conquistadors pushed up in the Inca empire, or the English vamped on India. The domination was obvious. But then came the missionaries, the laws, the State—the colonial culture. These caused the second, corresponding, aspect of patriarchy: *dependency*. The colonized were made to feel that they'd been chosen as subjects for a great, all encompassing, "civilizational" leap forward. That the invaders were sent by the "Great Father" in the sky, who'd sent word to the king, who in turn instructed the invaders to save the heathens from their wretched selves! Bring them into the modern world—by dint of cannon and bayonet if necessary:

> *Aristotle maintained that man's domination over animals extended to slaves and women as well, another view that mirrored the political reality of the day, since human slavery and subordination of women were the norm in Ancient Greece. In his* <u>Politics</u>, *Aristotle wrote that such "uncivilized" people as the neighboring Achaeans and Thracians "are slaves by nature, as the body is to the soul, or as beasts are to men." Aristotle believed it was as permissible to enslave people who did not possess "reason" as it was to enslave the common, and for the most part live at random.*[*]

---

[*] Henry Friedlander, *The Origins of Nazi Genocide: From Euthanasia to the Final Solution*, (Chapel Hill, University of North Carolina Press, 1995).

Legitimized thru Longevity

The same patriarchy which first oppressed women (after having perfected the methods on animals) as "inferiors," went on to evolve into the Judeo-Christian and Islamic institutions and theology that have scorched the planet today. This is why in every major religion god is a *he* or *him—Father*, i.e. *male* (according to "gender"). The last messenger, prophet, offspring and the last one god supposedly spoke to—yep, you guessed it, *men*. Coincidence? Natural? Not a chance. To make matters worse, as if patriarchy could even be content with one form of oppression, euro-supremacists went a step further than some unseen spirit in the sky, they painted a picture of their god-father's son in their image. They in effect became the prototype of the son of god's image and thus placed themselves in the direct lineage from god *himself*. Plato, Aristotle's teacher, created the idea of the "Great Chain of Being" which formalized the belief of the Greeks that they ranked higher than non-Greeks, women, slaves and of course animals.

> *Medieval Christendom translated Plato's image into a ladder which had God at the top and European Christian on the highest rung, a position that granted them a divine mandate as God's overseers and stewards to rule over the rest of the ladder below. The idea that European man flawed and sinful though he might be, occupied a position on earth comparable to God's position in the universe became a central idea in the religious and philosophical thought of Western civilization regarding man's place in nature. Thus Europeanism had virtually unlimited authority to rule the natural world as "the vice regent and deputy of almighty God."** *

---

* Patterson.

And because of this "virtual unlimited authority" there's a very dark, wretchedly oppressed and colonized woman in Bombay, with a picture of a prototypical European man on her wall who she believes is the son of god—her Lord and Savior—who died for *her* sins. Yet although he died for her "sins," she is still paying a perpetual debt she never owed. This scene is replicated a million times over across the globe in homes, hovels, huts, churches and prisons—in every colony.

The theocracies are heavily invested in the business of patriarchy—in domestication and colonization. And the colonial subjects respond with fealty and dependency. Women tell their sons to "be the man of the house." Men tell their wives to "stay in a woman's place." Men who show emotions are said to be "acting like little girls." Women who exert themselves as humans are called "dykes" and "bulldaggers" or "butch." Violence is masculinized and passivity is feminized. This is so because patriarchy has created two exclusive genders. Two neat little boxes to insert all of humanity. This has been legitimized by theocracy and capitalism thru longevity and a corresponding dependency by the masses on a grand distortion of nature itself.

The longevity We speak of here has to do with people divesting themselves of the responsibility of social investigation, of simply allowing abnormalities to persist without challenge because "it's always been this way" or "that's just the way it is." *No*, that's *not* just the way it is—it's the way it's been *made*. It hasn't fallen from the sky, or been miraculously blinked into existence. This oppression is man-made (literally)—it serves someone's interest. The people relinquish their power to oppression when they default on social investigation of curious and questionable systems. Patriarchy and its attendant ills slither on uninterrupted:

Patriarchy is a form of social organization that produces what we commonly recognize as sexism. But it goes well beyond individual or systemic prejudice against women. It is, first of all, the false division of all people into two rigid categories (male and female) that are asserted to be natural and moral. Patriarchy attempts to destroy, socially or even physically, anyone who does not fit into one of these categories or who rejects this "gender binary." Patriarchy goes on to define clear roles (economic, social, emotional, political) for men and women, and it asserts (falsely) that these roles are natural and moral. Under patriarchy, people who do not fit into or who reject these gender roles are neutralized with violence and ostracism. They are made to see and feel ugly, dirty, scary, contemptible, worthless. Patriarchy is harmful to everybody, and it is reproduced by everyone who lives with it. *

Weaponized Patriarchy

In addition to patriarchy going on to "define clear roles for men and woman," it also set in motion the ill definition of *races*. In creating itself first as a class of *men*, to domesticate and rule over animals, women and children, it was a logical progression of patriarchy to define all humans as being of different "races." For a plurality of races made it that much easier to justify, implement and sustain Plato's earlier design of the *Great Chain of Being*. Because patriarchy is necessarily hierarchical, it was but a short trip to the lunatic fringe of *racism*, though actually it was really euro-supremacy. To call it "racism" would, in essence, subtly reinforce

---

* Peter Gelderloos, *How Nonviolence Protects the State*, (South End Press, 2007).

the false social construct of a plurality of races on the planet. When, of course, this is not true. So, We'll call it what it is—euro-supremacy—and euro-supremacy is also euro-centricity.

Though, just as patriarchy is not exclusively a capitalist thing, nor is it exclusively a European thing. It's a man thing. It is highly contagious and must be combated constantly. It fastens a sense of entitlement that lends itself to taking liberties with other people's lives and existence based solely on what is perceived to be "difference." We focus our attention on euro-supremacy as an attendant ill/side-effect of patriarchy because it was them (English, French, Spaniards, Portuguese, Dutch, Belgians, etc.) who weaponized paternal relations in myriad conquests across the glove. It was the British empire upon whom it was said "the sun never set." In other words, its domination was global. And it is a fact that 99% of the borders between countries, nations and States were drawn by European colonialism.

What made euro-patriarchy weaponized, aside from the obvious, was that it created not only races of others, but made itself a race—a "white race" sitting atop the global food chain— the Great Chain of Being—doing their Father's work on earth. "Whites" polar opposite became, of course, the "blacks." Afrikans were made into the "black race." Asians became "yellow" and North American Indigenous nations became "red." Having already had a few centuries of practice domesticating animals, women and children in Europe, it was but a small tactical adjustment to train their cutlasses, ropes and cannons onto the "colored" people they encountered. The pivot was such that it needed only to hoist the same inferior attributes it used against its own people onto the Indigenous cultures it smothered. Everyone was demonized and maligned as "subhuman," "animalistic," "heathen" and in need of either elimination, colonization or paternalism. Genocide, oppression or protection (dependency). In any event, *all* encountered cultures had to come under the influence of euro-centric patriarchy. Which is to say the culture of the invaders—the crown, the religion, the laws. Social conditioning and gender placement was in essence the first human test run, the forerunner to, genetic engineering.

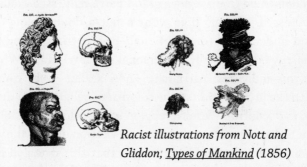

Racist illustrations from Nott and Gliddon, <u>Types of Mankind</u> (1856)

Grand Patriarchy

"People who do not fit into or who reject these gender roles are neutralized with violence and ostracized"—*Who* are the people who would reject these gender roles? Certainly they would be those who overstood patriarchy, colonialism, and who had a sense of self and kind so strong that they were deter-minded to assert themselves and be natural. Gender outlaws. Those who acted (and thought) outside of the box—the patriarchal gender box. However, when grand patriarchy came onto the scene, as a weaponized euro-supremacy, *all* Indigenous people, male and female, became *inferiors*.

Indigenous men were domesticated under grand patriarchy just as women had always been. And to insure this, a constant, blatant and open hostile state of terror and siege was used to blanket any notion to the contrary. Euro-supremacy smothered everything. Every male not a European became "boy," "buck," "son," or worse. They were explicitly forbidden to look a European male in the eyes. Grand patriarchy recognized one man—the European male. This was eventually utilized in the colonization of every encountered culture of the planet.

But not even this form of pervasive oppression eradicated patriarchy among those dominated. Oppressed men, those forbidden to be "men" under grand patriarchy, still would oppress oppressed women. Thus women felt a double blow of oppression under grand (on a national level) patriarchy and minor patriarchy—individually, in personal social relations. What's more is, this individual patriarchy—now sexism—was compounded with the introduction of the colonizers' religion into the mix as a chain of control. Western religion in the colonies became a "force-multiplier" for patriarchy. Another weapon used in the war. Once Indigenous men had been taught that this new god had given men dominion over women and children, these fell further down the *Great Chain of Being* (as created by Plato and reconfigured by Euro-Christians). Women, too, however, reciprocated this travesty by believing this foolishness to be true, making it that much easier for their oppression to continue.

But isn't it odd that the same religion that propelled the euro-supremacists out of Europe and against the world in a war-driven culture of conquest, made the people they encountered docile and meek? Instead of the Indigenous males using the bible to oppress women they could have used it to push back against the invaders... so what happened? It was perhaps the overwhelming military ability of that time. In any event, in a paradoxical twist, the colonized people reinforced the grand patriarchy with a spiritually ordained patriarchy of their own—even at the bottom rung of the ladder. Even under old colonialism where it is said that "Whole nations became as classes," the ills of patriarchy persisted and found expression. Though hardly to the extent it did on the grand level. Still...

Patriarchy in Neo-Colonialism

Class, gender, race and bourgeois law all stem from patriarchy. The illusion that men ("Father") knows best. To insure this doesn't escape anyone, man created religion in his image as well and endowed god with all the human attributes of a brutish man: jealousy, greed, vengeance, indifference, callousness and authoritarianism. When it's said that "god created man in his image," it's actually the reverse of that: *man created god in his image*. Class, gender, religion, race and bourgeois law—homophobia and heterosexism too—are all created of patriarchy. These, to look at it in another way, are the walls constructed in the global mansion of patriarchy to keep the Great Father safely sequestered away from those buried under the floor, in the closet, used as domestics, maintenance workers and beasts of burden.

To escape the gender box is, in essence, to become an outlaw of sorts. For one's escape from such restrictive confines is a *protest*—for one's ability to be natural. Out and away from the stifling confines of patriarchy's colonialism. But to protest is but one side of the equation. To protest is to go away from for self's sake. An overstandable thing. But to *rebel* is to go against the malady in an attempt to destroy it. Protests are usually nonviolent. A tactical method using hope as a morality play on power to have it change itself. Rebellion however is an active and often violent lunge at the power's heart to start the bleeding and stop the breathing. But even this is but a tactic and must be educated if the action is to bring about change.

Under old colonialism gender outlaws were smashed on by church and State. Sharp shooting ideologues riled up the masses to reject "ab-normality" for morals superior to such "deviance." Old colonialism, the general representative of patriarchy, used to push a line of gender authoritarianism. Even on a socio-economic level, old colonialism squatting dominantly over internal colonialism, however, has changed everything, but altered the perception of most things in order to continue to hold its empire together and reap benefits from oppression.

The u.s. ruling class has, in its new and enlightened age of neo-colonialism, come out as the main protector of civil rights against sexual, racial and religious discrimination. It bills itself as the force to make all "citizens" equal. Of course the paradox here is what We must focus on to find the truth. You see, because as the ruling class goes about claiming to be interested in protecting civil rights it is, in actuality, promoting and reinforcing patriarchy. It's the tactic of *problem-reaction-solution*. It's a Machiavellian ruse of traditional statecraft. Patriarchy created "gender" which begot sexism that leads to "sexual discrimination." Patriarchy created "race" which begot racism and leads to "racial discrimination." Patriarchy created religion—male dominated theocracies—which leads to "religious discrimination."

In other words, the very problems the masses are running to the State (representative of grand patriarchy) to solve, the State created and will then offer a solution to. Which, without question, will only strengthen the grip of patriarchy. It's the symbolic reapplication of the ties that bind which keep the masses tethered to the machine. Orwell anyone?

Patriarchal Contamination

Seated so close to the epicenter of empire, patriarchy and all that this entails, We are without question thoroughly contaminated. Cross-pollinated social interaction and conditioning has exposed us all to such a degree that We can hardly recognize our sickness. It all seems "normal" and "natural" doesn't it? That's because We've gone to the colonialist's schools, been socialized by its mass media, the propaganda of its many wars (even those against us), bourgeois elections, its culture of arrogance, smugness and indifference, etc. Because of this, and our inability to make sense of it, We act as unconscious shock troops of its colonial edicts when confronted with ideas and actions which appear to run counter to its mores. Being homophobic is one such thing. And of course racism is another. The animalized names the dominant culture has used to denigrate us all with We'll turn around and use on each other and ourselves to justify a sense of difference in imitation of patriarchy.

But you see, the neo (new) colonialism doesn't mind if its patriarchy is being imitated. That's a plus for it. That means it's working. It means people aren't trying to stop it, they are trying to like it. They don't want to *end* patriarchy, they want to be card carrying members of the club. Have you seen the ex-correctional officer, rapper Rick Ross, with his shirt off? The idiot has huge tattoos on his torso of u.s. currency—complete with Franklin's face, Jackson and Jefferson! He wants in so bad he's a walking billboard—"Will Beg For Membership." That's how patriarchy stays afloat and operable—by being legitimized, replicated and practiced by the unconscious masses. Neo-colonialism has found it expedient to ease up on the blatant authoritarianism and to let the colonial masses "do their thing." As long as it is within the established framework of the game—of bourgeois law and order.

So, while breaking out of the gender role is objectively wrong in the eyes of the patriarchy, it hasn't the time nor inclination to pursue such outlaws at this time. Actually, what the State has done under neo-colonialism is act as if it's okay and it has gone on the offensive trying to assure the people that all is well. First it was "smash on sight." Then it was "don't ask, don't tell." Now it's "come on in grab a gun and help defend the empire." Same way it did with New Afrikans, Mexicanos, Puerto Ricans and Indigenous nationals. 'Member that? Sure, it went like this: old colonialism, black codes, jim crow, segregation, civil rights and neo-colonialism—as integration. Those who refused to join the club were what? "Neutralized with violence and ostracized." Today We call them *martyrs, prisoners of war, political prisoners and exiles.* Those who joined We call neo-colonialists, petty bourgeois, sell-outs and collaborators—*enemies of the people.* The choice is now ours. What are We going to be? Projectiles *for* the people or projectiles *against* the people? That is the question.

Neo-colonialism has put the colonies on autopilot, and the masses have been confused by this, thinking that they are somehow on a flight towards freedom. Because the establishment forces aren't actively smashing on what used to be obvious causes for reaction, the people think a general sense of new freedom has blanketed the situation. Oprah has her own TV network, Jay Z wines and dines with Warren Buffet, Magic Johnson owns

COLONIALISM   NEO-COLONIALISM

the L.A. Dodgers and Rock Bottom is in the whitest house—but the usual reins of State control and reaction have not been relinquished, they've only been delegated to accommodating intermediaries to run the flight plan for the ruling class. The coordinates have been ⬛M5⬛ into the console, the flight is on autopilot, those the masses think are in control are only maintenance workers and sky marshals, flight attendants and observers, as the jumbo dreamliner continues uninterrupted across this neo-colonial terrain of war and class, amerikkkan style.

In this era of neo-colonialism the main homophobes are the masses themselves. Where it used to be the State, the church and other rabid ideologues of patriarchy, now it's athletes, rappers and the idiot down the tier who somehow feels as if *his* so-called "manhood" is threatened by how or who another person lives and loves. The unconscious shock troops of patriarchy become gatekeepers for their oppressors. That's why patriarchy can feel so comfortable with putting the colonies on auto-pilot. The inmates have assumed control of the asylum and all is well on the western front. Never mind that the very culture of oppression that they are holding up by becoming little oppressors themselves is the actual threat to them. It's an *Animal Farm* trip, really. Or a Stockholm syndrome type of situation. Where the entity doing you the harm you side step to attack the one on your side—while loving your tormentor. Psych meds, anyone?

Mark Carson, a New Afrikan gay man, was murdered on May 17, 2013.

Harmful to Everybody

To overstand homophobia and heterosexism as oppressive tools of the patriarchy is to come to grips with one's own reality. A reality that shouts its existence not from the confines of your own head or intellect—or even your culture. It's a reality put on you by an offending order of parties who wish only to control and exploit you to their delight and benefit. Those "shouts of reality" We speak of are from a distance of centuries past, and their antiquity gives them an air of prestige and legitimacy, but you mustn't be fooled. For this is the culture that ripped apart your ancestors— this is it. It's shinier now, has more pixels and is in high definition, but it is the same culture that pushed up on those shores and was mistaken as god. It is the very same system of control, too. The gatekeepers' complexions have changed—We can see the madness thru the lens of BET and Univision now instead of just CBS and NBC, but look carefully and listen, it's still the same old thing—patriarchy, class, gender, race, colonialism. The slings and arrows aimed at gender outlaws today are the same ones that were flung at us when patriarchy first drove up. We were the abnormal ones then. And now, what, We've become so "normal" (amerikan) that We are oppressors, too? We've been amerikanized to the point where We can't even recognize We aren't even ourselves anymore. Yeah, "amerikkkan me."

In men's prison—where as prisoners, the only women are transwomen—the concentration of the patriarchy pathology is on steroids. Even in those prisons without transwomen,

*New Afrikan transwoman
CeCe McDonald, sent to prison in 2012
for defending herself against a racist,
transphobic attack in Minneapolis.*

as patriarchy is also homophobia and heterosexism, it finds expression in this way. Whether thru predation or hate outright, ill vibrations play out against gays or trans prisoners as, invariably, they are referred to as "punk," "faggots," "bitches," etc. The hierarchical structure of prison groups preclude any form of socialization or respect with, or towards, gay prisoners. They are treated as "abnormals"—as less than human. They are usually "neutralized with violence and ostracized." Groups forbid their members from aiding any such person. And even though the prisoners are placed with nationals from oppressed and colonized nations, oppression and prejudice against gays and trans prisoners goes on uninterrupted as patriarchal "morals" are imitated and replicated across the board.

The odd thing, though one which points up the patriarchal reality in vivid fashion, is in most prison cultures the only party in a gay encounter that's considered gay is the one assuming the so-called passive or feminine role. The masculine one, the top, is considered "the man," which somehow excludes him from being gay or bi. It's his prerogative to fuck something, huh? And, much like sexism out in Babylon where the woman is considered lesser than, so too it is in prison with the gay or transgender prisoner. Though more so, since the homophobia and heterosexism is driven by the "morals" of religion. Of course, patriarchy escapes mention altogether. Nevertheless, the pathology of patriarchy plays itself out even in the most oppressive situations imaginable.

The fact of the matter is, We can talk about this until We

New Afrikan transwoman
Brandy Martell, murdered on
April 29, 2012, in a transphobic
attack in Oakland, CA.

are out of breath, but until gays and transgender prisoners, and people at large, take their lives and existence into their own hands, organize and defend their reality, they'll continue to be victimized and exploited. That goes for any form of oppression. The oppressed have the responsibility to get free. Freedom is not given or granted—it's *taken!* The federal government is not going to legislate your safety into existence. The prison administration cannot—nor will it—protect you from hostile homophobes or predators. You have to organize yourselves in concert with methods that reflect your reality. We know that in the state prison at Walla Walla, in Washington, the revolutionary comrades organized Men Against Sexist Shit (MASS) to combat homophobia and heterosexism there.

Revolutionaries should be on the front lines of combating all forms of oppression. We have to organize with the oppressed to strike for freedom or the neo-colonialists will organize. Them against us, and continue on.

To Be Like...

To be a lapdog of u.s. imperialism you have to be like mindless soldiers who voluntarily sign up to oppress other poor people. You have to be a mindless entertainer—while on BET you floss a street swag in an attempt to fool the youth into believing you are in the same position as them—then you run off to the whitest house to do a Motown revue or put on the lights of a Christmas tree, where you rub elbows with other collaborators and oppressors smiling, soft shoeing and doing your best impression of "high culture."

To be kept safe and alive, out of harm's way and in front of cameras as a weapon of mass destruction, you have to act angry. As if you have a real issue, while promoting foreign cars, exotic jewelry, expensive liquor, outrageous fashions and naked women. You have to coat your body in a gaggle of meaningless tattoos, throw up a gang-less sign and frown menacingly through some obnoxious, face altering sunglasses. You have to mention guns, sexual prowess, hate, obsessions with the inane (absurd); you have to flail your arms wildly and do a two-step walk that resembles a war-dance from a street org you're not a member of nor would ever be considered for. You'll need to cover your natural teeth with metal and glass sold to you by the oppressors of your people.

You'll have to do all this under the watchful eyes of a security firm that keeps those you're trying to fool at a safe distance—lest they test your gangster and realize that it is *not* what it is. To prevent this occurrence you'll be better off doing your video in the safe confines of a studio in front of a green screen where images can later be computer-generated onto it.

What you can't do, however, is mention the following:

→ National Oppression
→ Patriarchy
→ Homophobia
→ Capitalism
→ Neo-Colonialism
→ Protracted People's War
→ Socialism
→ Communists
→ Revolutionary Nationalism
→ The Black Liberation Army
→ Imperialism
→ Liberation of Political Prisoners
→ Self-determination

Or that Obama is an Uncle Tom to the 10th power, and a Zionist.

In other words, you can floss in Tom Foolery all day on *106 & Park*. You do know that BET is owned by CBS? That CBS is one of the major propaganda pillars of the settler government and thus the bourgeoisie?

As long as you employ the meaningless formula of fluff, pomp, posture and posing, you can stay *106 & Park* countdown for 19, 20 weeks. As long as you promote collaboration, parasitism, black-american-ism, a willingness to be angry *within* the established boundaries of colonial legality, you're touted as a star. You know the business: anger, undirected rage—pseudo-struggle.

From your infantry work distracting New Afrikan youth—once you've proven worthy in this regard—you'll be promoted up the chain (literally) as a small bit actor in hood movies; then independent films and maybe even a major motion picture. And, if your show/act is that believable, you could get a position on a TV drama as—*of course*—a pig. And let's be clear, whether you portray a detective, a navy investigator, or a medical examiner—that's all *pig*. You are an entertainer in a business that promotes, supports and contains national oppression.

In your pursuit of money (which you've been led to believe is freedom—which you are now trying to make others believe) you've been played all the way out of pocket. Now they got you singing and dancing at memorials for imperialist troops killed in colonialist actions. They'll move you onto the country music circuit, a New Year's celebration in N.Y., a tour of duty in the hoods and barrios to promote participation in bourgeois elections; in defense of charter schools that promote nothing but dependency and white supremacy. They'll parade you on *Extra*, *Entertainment Tonight* and *Good Morning Amerika*. They'll have you begging your nation for money to support the victims of the earthquake, tsumani, and radiation leak in one city of rich ass Japan while down the street Mrs. Johnson can't afford to eat and also pay for her medication. Support one city in Japan while your *whole* nation is under a genocidal tsunami. Good work, idiot.

Another video, another tattoo, another chain, another car, another half-naked dance—another stitch in this satin lining of the national coffin. You're not significant enough to be a nail in the coffin—don't fool yourself. You're only a small thread, a mere stitch, in the lining. That is all. The thing is however, there's no shortage of you bastards. But trust and believe—the revolutionaries are coming!

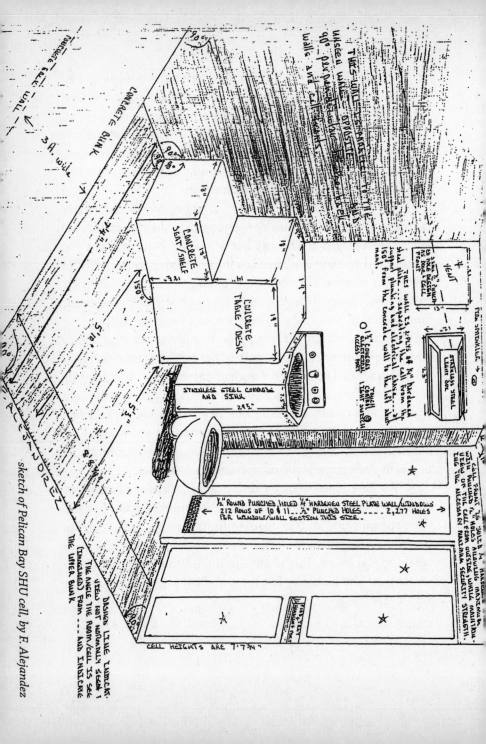

sketch of Pelican Bay SHU cell, by F. Alejandez

The Reverse Nuremberg Defense
*Or The Robot Defense**

After the second imperialist war, in which the u.s., France and Britain smashed on Italy, Japan and Germany, the victors put on a show trial in Nuremberg, Germany, where a clutch of Nazi functionaries were tried for war crimes, convicted and subsequently hanged or shot. (To be fair, however, some were acquitted and others given lengthy prison sentences and spared the death penalty.)

The defense presented invariably by those soldiers and functionaries on trial, was "I was only following orders." In essence, kicking the responsibility for their actions and obvious atrocities up the chain of command to their superiors. Arguing that had the orders not been given to do as they had, the atrocities would never have occurred. Further, they stressed, that their outfits were such that the complex bureaucracy prevented any actions that were not explicitly ordained from the top. This defense entered the public domain, or stream of human consciousness (the matrix), and has since become known as "The Nuremberg Defense." E.g. *I was only following orders.*

---

* Written three days before our first hungerstrike (7-1-11) after trying to move various criminal elements into active resistance against the general indeterminate status. Surprisingly, most in the vicinity complied. Enough to make the hungerstrike in the long corridor successful.

Apparently the Nuremberg Defense has trickled down even into the often cutthroat and chaotic stocks of criminality. However, as is often the case in such things, the already weak and feeble defense has been perverted further—inverted actually and turned on its head and utilized as an excuse to not act in one's own best interests. It's a strange phenomenon to observe, as ones who professed to be "in resistance," "conscious" or "about struggle," do fantastic, mind boggling acts of knee-jerk gymnastics to justify why they in fact cannot support an action that would serve the interests of all involved—including themselves. But as the contradiction of our oppression here in the SHU sharpens, those who are about absolutely nothing are being exposed as the reactionaries that they've always been. That in spite of all the hard words they use in their points, bylaws and whatever, they are about nothing. Well, that's not altogether true. They are about something, but it's just totally reactionary, anti-people and collaborationist.

Here's the thing, We are collectively locked in the SHU—indefinitely. We have SHU terms without any rules violations. In fact, a prisoner can literally murder another prisoner in the general population and only be given a five year SHU term. Once his/her five years is up he/she will be let back out to the mainline. However, if the same prisoner is found with a birthday card signed by fellow prisoners, with say, an Indigenous number (two bars and three dots) then that is going to be used as a "point" towards giving that prisoner a life term in the SHU. Similarly, if the prisoner is found with study and struggle material from Comrade George Jackson, or some Kiswahili or Nahuatl—these are points to be lodged against the prisoner as the authoritarian gang investigators [sic] go about their so-called "investigation" to *validate* the prisoner in question.

Of course, once one is validated by having the so-called "three points" which somehow "prove" one's membership in or association with a prison org, he/she can come up for an "inactive/active" review every six years. One year longer for a mere review than a prisoner who murdered another prisoner would do before getting *out* of the SHU.

So, for learning about one's culture, its Indigenous language, its revolutionaries and national identity (i.e. politics), one is set upon by the political police, the Institutional Gang Investigators (IGI), and whisked off to one of the three SHU's operating in the state or left for years on end in one of the Administrative Segregation Units (ASU's) waiting to be sent to a SHU.

The height of repression, in its most crystallized form and nakedness, is the SHU here at Pelican Bay. And within its already repressive confines of listless solitary are the wicked doldrums of the short corridor. Four blocks, on the D-Facility side. For those there it's a constant struggle to maintain a sense of self and collective awareness. For those not yet in those blocks it's a slow-motion psychological torture session as one waits to be told to "Roll your property up you're being moved." It's akin to cattle being slowly moved towards the electrified cattle prod and slaughter. They know that the cow that was near them is *now* gone—moved and never to be seen again. Two or three times a month prisoners are plucked from among us to be "moved"—We all know where they are being sent and why. The short corridor for maximum repression.

So, the collective call has come out of this kamp that We have an obligation to ourselves, our nations, our cultures, to resist this authoritarian reign of terror. That regardless of what your particular politics are the hammer is upon us all as prisoners here in the SHU on indeterminate status. As one comrade said, "Today it's us, but tomorrow it will be you." A general call was issued and those connected made the effort to make those in the immediate vicinity aware of the issues. Words came through from other countries—this is how tight the security under here is—words on the general effort were transmitted via other countries to us before words made it across the kamp grapevine. Nevertheless, the words and issues were received, given to those in the same condition as everyone else—some words were even particularly spelled out—and yet as if in a bad comedy some prisoners said: "We haven't gotten any word on it"!?

The Nuremberg Defense was inverted from "I was following orders" to "I was given no orders." One has been reduced to a mere robot in essence. Capable of working in one's defense only when someone is programming it or stroking its keys. Here's the analogy We're working with: someone is drowning, flailing his/her arms wildly, when all of a sudden it dawns on him/her that, "Hey, no one told me to try to save myself! i didn't get the word to resist an obvious death, to get to a dry spot and save myself and perhaps save someone else who, in the future, may end up almost drowning." Sounds crazy, doesn't it?

But of course it's deeper than that. If it were only that simple We might be able to get past this with some degree of overstanding. However, things have a materialist basis in reality and as much as We'd like to sometimes think otherwise, things don't mysteriously fall from the sky. How is it that We've been so biased against our own survival? Let's look at this for a minute because it may prove fruitful in our future endeavors as the contradictions sharpen and the struggles intensify.

We're not talking about going out into, say, a working-class area and trying to convince the proletariat about the evils of capitalism—about the inherent oppression in colonialism—where people have hotdogs, baseball, apple pie and chevrolet to distract them from their awful lot. No, nothing that complex. We're talking about prisoners who are in the SHU without having ever violated a rule, *forever* (indeterminate) and subjected to the most inhumane conditions imaginable—who languish at the absolute bottom of a totally antagonistic and hostile society. We're talking about prisoners who are in the hole for exerting their culture and national identity. But... We are talking about humans—the material beings that exist inside of nature—who, in spite of being at the very last and lowest rung of a class-based society, have their own set of internal contradictions and dynamics that create motion, that ultimately drive interests. We are talking about criminals (parasites) who have colonial (petty bourgeois) mentalities. Which is to say, a non-revolutionary class that depends largely upon the working class for its sustenance. And by colonial mentality what is meant is that one recognizes the legitimacy of the settler government and its rules. Regardless of whether one breaks the rules—one still ultimately and objectively believes in the inherent right of the bourgeois State to govern them and oppress their nation. To not struggle to end oppression is to legitimize it through inactivity.

With the hunger strike that's looming, some prisoners—mainly those who are the most reactionary, i.e. those who are stuck watching go-nowhere programs on TV all day; those who read nothing more serious than a novel and those who can't string together an intelligent or thought-provoking sentence either verbally or in writing—conversely, these are the someones who'll dominate the tier for hours with a litany of absurd jokes and mindless intrigues about things that have absolutely no bearing on real life—it's these loud, often braggadocious reactionaries who have led the charge in inverting the Nuremberg Defense. Those who in spite of their tough demeanor in the safe confines of their cells obviously don't really want to go to the mainline. Don't want the protest against the indeterminate status that may get us all back out into general population. And here We come across a glaring contradiction that needs to be expounded upon.

There are some, if not most, who only know prison as the SHU. Some prisoners were validated in reception, before even getting to any mainline. Their whole prison experience has been nothing but single cell living in eight cell pods, on walk-alone yards. Human contact consisting of momentary finger bumps through the heavy industrial metal slab covering the cells.* These prisoners know only handcuffed escorts and ten-minute showers three times a week. Visits through the thick plexiglass windows under the never-blinking eye of a camera. To them this all seems "normal," "regular," "just the way it is"—and, to be frank, it offers a perverted sense of "i'm tough" to the young prisoner. Creating the illusion for him that all this is to contain him and that this somehow proves his toughness.

On the flipside, of course, there's the convicts who over-stand that all this is nothing. These are the men who've been in Old Folsom, San Quentin, Soledad, Tracy and New Folsom; those who've seen and felt the actual power of prisoners. Who, for what-ever reason, have been with the herd and know that this here... all this single-cell, walk-alone, eight-cell-pod-living and escorts is not a consequence of anyone's toughness or one's badness. On the contrary, it's a sign of our collective weakness. Dialectically, our weakness means the pigs' strength. That's how that works. Convicts used to run prisons. Not anymore. Yes, those who are in prison have been "convicted"—but to be a *convict* is another animal altogether. Don't want to waste too much time on this.

---

* "Finger bumping" is what We do under here for human contact. See, the cells are industrial steel plates across the front with 2,800 finger-tip-size holes drilled into them. So, in lieu of a handshake or a hug, We touch fingertips—finger bump. Yeah, it leaves *a lot* to the imagination, but it's all We got. It's a desperate move to at least have some form of human contact.

Prisoners have grown complacent in the maintenance of their social structure. This kamp, Pelican Bay, has without question taken its toll upon us. However, We are still committed—or at least should be—to the breathing. Some, however, have allowed the appearance of being tough to impede their recognition of struggling against the conditions that are grinding us into dust and simultaneously struggling for the very things that ultimately allow us to hold our heads up, chests out, backs straight. Those who have pulled out and then inverted the Nuremberg Defense are out of pocket. They are comfortable under here where they are safe, individualistic and have no responsibility other than a morning and evening roll-call or gossiping through a steel door to the next pod.

The real convicts, those who know and have experienced collective struggle, die lonely deaths of the spirit daily under all this isolation. Knowing in their heart of hearts that this is no big display of our toughness. Fortitude yes, in withstanding the years of this desolate living, but that one's criterion for toughness is to mingle and move with the herd. To affect change in a collective setting where conflicts can be challenged and resolved in appropriate settings. That's what the righteous do.

So, in closing, i am just trying to make the courageous aware that those who ain't really about nothing will ultimately do nothing. And have furthermore rejected the idea under the upside-down Nuremberg Defense. The path of least resistance has always been chosen by the faint of heart. The State has taken the initiative in this struggle to destroy us all. It is up to us to wrest that initiative back from them and save ourselves. By doing so We save others from a similar fate.

MONSTER

THE AUTOBIOGRAPHY OF AN L.A. GANG MEMBER

"A shockingly raw, frightening portrait of gang life in South Central Los Angeles today."
—MICHIKO KAKUTANI, *The New York Times*

SANYIKA SHAKUR, aka
MONSTER KODY SCOTT

To: Warden of Pelican Bay-SHU
From: Sanyika Shakur, D#07829/C-7-112
Re: Banned Publication

Dear Sir,
It has recently been brought to my attention that my first book, *Monster: The Autobiography of an L.A. Gang Member* (Grove/Atlantic, 1993), has been added to the ever growing list of banned and otherwise restricted books allowed in Pelican Bay's Security Housing Unit.

This list includes, but is not exhausted, by the likes of:

Blood In My Eye & *Soledad Brother*—George Jackson
The War Before—Safiya Bukhari
Guerrilla Warfare—Che Guevara
Defying The Tomb—Kevin Rashid Johnson
Mein Kampf—Adolf Hitler

With the exception of Hitler, i'd say i was actually keeping good company. However, that's not the point of this letter. In fact, this letter is being sent to you in order to make a request—a mere suggestion, if you will.

You see, i've had an indeterminate SHU term since September of 1989. Validated as a threat to the safety and security of the institution for associating with revolutionaries. I was brought to Pelican Bay in March of 1990. It was, in fact, from this very SHU that i penned the book you have now banned—and, i might add, it was a phenomenal bestseller here in the empire, as well as in ten outlying nations across the globe. Not bad actually since i never completed school beyond the 6th grade. Actually, my source of growth, development and awareness came by studying some of the authors you've also found fit to ban and exclude. Well, that is, with the exception of Hitler, for obvious reasons.

Yes, well, more to the point... You see, i was afforded the opportunity to read the memo which instructed staff and prisoners alike that *Monster* was being banned because it "promotes violence and anti-government behavior." It said that *Monster* was "anti-staff and not in accord with legitimate penological interests." Was, in fact, "hostile and revolutionist in nature." And for these reasons it would "not be allowed in Pelican Bay SHU."

Sir, you'll forgive me here if i come across as a little slow on the uptake, but things seem a bit confusing at this point. Well, you'll see, this brings me to my suggestion/request—of which, given the circumstances, outlining your valiant efforts to bring this environment into accord with "penological...." nay, "*legitimate* penological interests*," and all—you must know and overstand that *Monster* is a book. A book made of paper, bound by threads and glue. That it contains cold black type. Oh, sure there's a photo on its cover of me with an automatic weapon, but that is but a two dimensional image—easily removed.

Here's what i suggest—a mere humble request from down here in the cellblocks where We languish in the throes of suspended animation, more dead than alive: since i am a "revolutionist," am "hostile" and "anti-government," and since i don't believe in the use of solitary confinement as punishment or as a means of reform—you may as well mark me down as being against your "legitimate penological interests," too—given these reasons, as a living, breathing and thinking human (unlike a dead tree book), why don't you issue a memo banning *me* from the Security Housing Unit in Pelican Bay!?

Think about it.

"Objectively, the Situation with Me and These Pigs is Political"

QUESTION: We are sitting here with Comrad-Brother Sanyika Shakur of the August 3rd Collective, a conscious citizen of the Republic of New Afrika, and a newly released survivor of the Pelican Bay Security Housing Unit. We are conducting this interview on behalf of the comrades at Kersplebedeb Book Publishing and Distribution. Welcome, Sanyika.

SANYIKA: Thank you. Asante.

QUESTION: During your time in prison as a young man you wrote your bestselling book *Monster, Autobiography of an L.A. Gang Member*. You were released, and then several years later in 2007 your name was put on LAPD's list of the ten most wanted gang members and you ended up back at Pelican Bay. Can you tell us what happened?

SANYIKA: Well, first and foremost i'd like to send a clenched fist salute to the comrades at Kersplebedeb for taking time out to interview me and all the comrades in struggle from coast to coast across the planet. Fighting imperialism is not terrorism!

The situation with me and the LAPD has always been antagonistic. When i was a criminal it was antagonistic, but more so when i became political. After i wrote *Monster* in '93, the situation became antagonistically political in the sense that they saw that—not just LAPD but just pigs, period, reactionaries—they felt, and rightfully so, that i had made a transition, that i had turned a corner and became more of a threat than i ever could be as a criminal.

So as a consequence of that awareness on their behalf they intensified their effort to destroy me. They did that in various ways, by engaging me several times in attempts to murder me. However, i've always been resilient and have always struggled against their attempts, and up until this point have always emerged victorious.

Without going into all the details—because if i did they'd likely try to get me on a parole violation—i can say this: an individual came to me with an offer to buy a car, the car was purchased, and then six months later he reported the car stolen. For making the transgression of inviting the pigs into our personal dealings, he was disciplined, and as opposed to him accepting his discipline he ran to the amerikan security forces and said that i had taken the car from him and in fact had beat him. Needing no prompting, LAPD the reactionary pigs that they are, went right into motion: they charged me with carjacking, they said it was burglary because i took him into a dwelling where he was disciplined, they said he suffered great bodily injury as a consequence of a broken eye socket, and they said i robbed him though nothing was supposedly taken but the car.

Pig press conference announcing capture of Sanyika Shakur in 2007.

i was immediately put on an FBI/LAPD taskforce list of ten most wanted gang members. They haven't registered me as a gang member in over twenty years, but this is the list that they already had compiled, so they just put me on the list up there as a consequence of who i am. i was just a target of opportunity. And there began the hunt: $50,000 reward, for not even my conviction but just my capture, so it didn't take long for informants to lead them to me. i was captured on March 7, 2007, in South Central; i got 6 years with 85%, that was the plea bargain. i had to plead to carjacking as a consequence of the individuals who were captured in the car—not myself, two other individuals—who said that i gave them the car. As a consequence of having an indeterminate SHU since 1989—meaning that i'm saddled with a validation, that i've been deemed a threat to the institutional security of the California Department of Corrections (CDC)—they kept me in the hole. This was how i ended up back in Pelican Bay.

2007 wasn't the only time i've ended up back in Pelican Bay. i initially got out of Pelican Bay in 1995, after having written *Monster* in '93. i was recaptured in '96 for a brawl with three parole agents, which i won. i was captured in '97 for going to New York without permission, i was given a 90 day violation. i was recaptured again in '98 for two attempted murders on the LAPD, two assaults with deadly weapons on the LAPD: they attacked me, i won, they filed charges. In 2001, i was recaptured. It's been a series of captures, hunts, consequences, clashes, collisions with me and u.s. law enforcement as a consequence of my steadfast refusal to bow down.

Objectively, the situation with me and these pigs is political; and politics is war without bloodshed and war is politics with bloodshed—it's all politics. That's what the situation with me and these pigs is. Because i haven't committed a criminal act against a working-class person since i was a member of a street organization. Since i've been a member of the New Afrikan Independence Movement, a conscious citizen of the Republic of New Afrika, i've committed no transgressions against any proletariat, any working-class person, student or elder.

QUESTION: Pelican Bay Security House Unit, also known as the SHU, has been described by prisoners and outside observers alike as a torture unit where prisoners are subjected to long-term isolation. Could you describe life in the SHU?

SANYIKA: It's stark—it's stark, it's quiet, it's sterile, it's concrete, it's cold—it's without question the end of the line, and they make no qualms about that being what it is. It is actually what it is: it's the end of the line.

It's a two-tier situation: a bottom tier with four cells in it, a top tier with four cells in it. The four cells are about 8 by 10, two concrete bunks, a stainless steel toilet/sink combination, and that's it. A makeshift desk, but it's not practical for writing; a very thin mattress; you get two blankets, you get two jumpsuits, you get four pairs of socks, two t-shirts, two boxers, one pair of shoes. You can have ten books or you can have ten magazines. You can have five books or five magazines. You can have one ink pen filler—not an ink pen, an ink pen filler: you have to wrap paper around the ink filler in order to write. Now you can spend up to $55 at the canteen once a month, but they take everything out of the bags and put it into brown paper bags as a consequence of what they call security.

Pelican Bay, it's torture insomuch as the isolation is permanent. We used to be allowed to have cellies in the early '90s when i first got there. i first got there in 1990, February 1990. We were allowed to have cellies beginning in April. Though conditions in the kamp drove prisoners to the point where they felt in '97, '98, and '99 that there had to be a cleaning of house, so i think that eleven or twelve people were killed by their cellies. That put an end to us having cellmates which then drove us further into isolation and solitary because when you're in the cell with someone you tend to have human contact, you can talk to someone quietly, you can exchange ideas. But as a consequence of the murders—which were a consequence of the conditions—We were driven further into isolation by being put into a solitary situation.

Pelican Bay is their answer to prison unity, it's their answer to prison legality, it's their answer to prison reform, it's their answer to an alternative power source, it's their answer to revolutionary consciousness. Twelve years before they opened up Guantanamo Bay they opened up Pelican Bay—that shouldn't be lost on anyone.

It is torture insomuch as there is no vocational/technical training, very little religious activity sponsored by the State or any outside group. It's just a long continuum of nothing. The food is the same every day: We get no salt, We get no pepper, We get no sugar. They cut the tops of our cakes off, We just get the spongy bottom. We get the same lunch every day. The water is lukewarm. We shower every other day if there's no lockdown. We can go to a little makeshift yard every day for 90 minutes if you please, but you get no recreational equipment and it's just another cell, except there's no roof but a steel grate with a plastic top on top of it with cameras sticking through.

You're just left there to vegetate if you have no means to support yourself by an adequate library from comrades. If comrades weren't sending in materials to us, more of us would have vegetated, because Pelican Bay is bent on the breaking, the mind-warping, and the rebuilding of prisoners in the image of what CDC deems appropriate. So, it's a torture chamber no doubt. It's designed to break us down and then rebuild us in the image of what's conducive to "penological" progress, which of course means in our language: oppression.

QUESTION: Who ends up in the SHU?

SANYIKA: First of all let me say this: there are no gangs in Pelican Bay SHU; that's a tricky euphemism, it's semantics that CDC uses. While prisoners at Pelican Bay did or had on the street belonged to street organizations/"gangs", once people become permanent prisoners or long-term prisoners in any level 4 or level 3 setting the gang situations cease to exist and it becomes a matter of organizational activity. This organizational activity creates an alternative power source that CDC does not want to exist, so what they do is they create language that implies criminal activity and then their response to criminal activity is to isolate these individuals with the excuse that "they're gang members, they're members of prison gangs" or "they're associates of prison gangs." These words "prison" and "gang" are designed to get a reaction, and then the public says "Well that's all they're putting in these places, prison gang members. They haven't learned their lesson on the street and now they're even in prison being in gangs." And that's not the case.

Who ends up in Pelican Bay? First and foremost those who have decided consciously to go another way, away from the established system, to try to eradicate that system and to rebuild. So what i'm saying is revolutionaries end up there. Prisoners with social consciousness end up there. Jailhouse lawyers, those who help other prisoners with litigation to appeal their sentences, they end up there. The interesting thing about Pelican Bay is, you can kill another prisoner in general population and the max you can get in the hole is 5 years, 60 months. You can kill another prisoner, take his or her life and end up with 60 months in the hole, but if you get caught with one of George Jackson's books or some Swahili or some Nahuatl or something by Magon or Che or if you have a certain tattoo—a dragon, a star, two bars, three dots—if you show any sign of resistance you will end up in Pelican Bay. What they'll say is you are a threat to the institutional security.

A case in point: on August 11th, i was still a threat to the institutional security so i couldn't go out to the main population, the general population with other prisoners. i was deemed a threat to other prisoners and staff—and yet on August 12, Black August, i was standing in Home Depot surrounded by civilians. That they let me out onto the street, but they wouldn't let me around other "criminals," the contradiction of that blows in the face of their whole security trip.

The prison-industrial-complex is a racket. It's just another big business venture sponsored by, for, and to the advantage of capitalism. And prisons are designed, especially for the internal nations, as genocidal stockades. While you'll get a few people in there for stabbings and things like that, for the most part the people who end up in Pelican Bay are those who resist, those who have shown a distinct effort to revolutionize the consciousness of other prisoners, those who demonstrate legal acumen. Pelican Bay and Corcoran state prison are designed to break political people—and politics are any relations between people centered on the seizure and retention of State power, so politics are vast. That's what Pelican Bay does.

QUESTION: How do people cope in the SHU?

SANYIKA: Well, not everybody can. And people retreat into madness continuously. We hear it over the tiers a lot. What they used to do in the early '90s, is they would just throw anybody in there, and so prisoners who already had a history of psychosis or had mild situations of schizophrenia or paranoia would immediately fall all the way off. They would begin to rub feces on themselves, throw urine, antagonize other prisoners. Then in the *Madrid* ruling, Judge Thelton Henderson of San Francisco said that Pelican Bay was indeed cruel and usual punishment, but as the prison population was so vast and the people in Pelican Bay were so few that at the expense of these few to save the rest of these people, We can keep them in there. However, those with psychological problems, after *Madrid* they put them in the PSU, the Psychological Service Unit. That relieved the pressure on other prisoners from the clashes that would occur as a consequence of some individual going off and losing his mind.

The coping mechanisms that i used in Pelican Bay were study and struggle. A constant repetition of study and struggle. And what i mean by that is, not just reading, but study: reading, consuming, meditating, thinking. Once you get to that stage then you begin to struggle around the issue. Whether it's how do We implement a socialist system, how do We bring back sister- and brotherhood, or how do We formulate a people's army. These are all issues that We have to implement as a consequence of our study and struggle.

That was my particular coping mechanism. i knew that they were trying to break me and so that gave me a determination to not be broken, which then led me to reach out. And i reached out to other comrades, and not just the New Afrikan Independence Movement, but i went out to Canada, i went to New York, i went to Germany, i went to Ireland. i started reaching out to revolutionaries across the planet and they in turn responded and began to support the efforts that they saw me engaged in, which was study and struggle. And so my thing was to bear down and use what i learned to try to aid someone else from falling into the traps that i had fallen into and moreso getting up out of that trap. Breaking loose and correcting the person that made me trapped.

All that is interconnected, the coping mechanisms are various. Each individual has his or her own ways of dealing with it. You know, exercise: i walk continuously up and down the cell, i meditate. Like i said, i study, i struggle, i write. i stay in communication with people so i try to have a constant stream of letters coming in and going out, and i try and let people know that although i'm buried alive i'm still struggling. My coping mechanism was socializing, as much as i could.

QUESTION: When were you first held in Pelican Bay?

SANYIKA: In 1989, in September, i was given my final point: it takes three points to be given what's called indeterminate or to be validated. So i got my third point in 1989: they said i had written a letter with revolutionary overtones. That landed me in Ad-Seg in Soledad. When i got to Ad-Seg, they had a situation, a group of people there called CAC, Criminal Activities Coordinator, which is IGI (Institutional Gang Investigations). They went through their investigation and they said in 1988 i had been observed exercising in military fashion with known revolutionaries in Folsom Prison, and then in 1987 they said while in San Quentin i had received some writings by Comrade George Jackson that someone had sent me through the mail. i never got it, they intercepted it; they never told me they had intercepted it, nor did they tell me they had taken pictures of me and these revolutionaries exercising in Folsom in '88. Well in '89 when i came back they had started the new Pelican Bay validation program, and i already had two points. So when they said i had written a letter with revolutionary overtones in '89, that was my third and final point. That in effect gave me life in the hole.

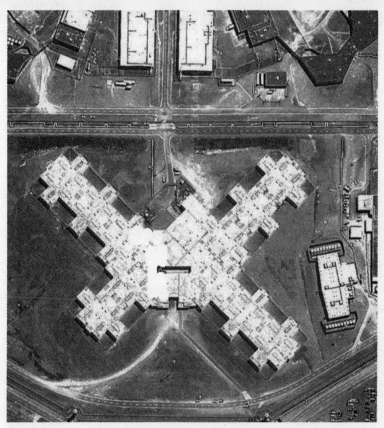

There's three long sides and one short side, and the short side is just four buildings on one corridor. Four blocks, 1 through 4, that's what's called the short corridor. On the other hallway of D facility there's 5 through 10, and on C facility side there's 12 blocks: 1 through 6 on one corridor and 7 through 12 on the other corridor.

So these three are called long corridors and then there's the short corridor. The short corridor is designed for people who have life, who are validated and are considered cadre, people who are active, and obviously can't be broken and have been at the height and at the top of the game of struggle while in prison.

And so from September 4th, 1989, at various times i've been in both Ad-Seg and Pelican Bay. i've gone through Corcoran twice, the first time was in '91 when i stayed there for 6 months on a layaway waiting to go back to Pelican Bay. That was during the height of the cockfights (the staged fights between prisoners that the pigs would set up). i went back through there in 1999–2000 for another 6 month stay and then back to Pelican Bay.

QUESTION: In 2011 prisoners in the SHU organized a hunger strike against their conditions and against the gang validation policies, which eventually rallied support in prisons throughout California with over six thousand prisoners refusing food. How did the strike go down in Pelican Bay?

SANYIKA: July 1st, the word had came down from the comrades in the short corridor that We should begin to implement ways in which to roll back the draconian issue of our gang validation. The hunger strike was built around five core demands and the most important of these had to do with the gang validation, with people who debrief, and with the lack of any fair impartial hearing during investigations. These five demands came down from the comrades on the short side.*

By that time We had been in the hole for 20 years, for political reasons. We had not earned our way into this hole for having stabbed or knocked down a couple of pigs. We were not there because We corrected a rapist or corrected a child molester, or an informant. In my case, i got life in the hole because they said i

---

* "Debriefing" refers to CDCR's demand that prisoners turn informant before being released from the SHU. Abolishing the debriefing policy was a key demand in 2011 and 2013. For a list of the Five Core Demands of the 2011 California hungerstrike, see Appendix 1.

exercised with revolutionaries, because i wrote a letter that they said had revolutionary overtones, and that i had writings from comrade George Jackson. That is what got me the rest of my life in the hole, deemed a threat to the institutional security.

So We always knew that it was politics—bourgeois politics, reactionary politics—so We got together. We had had a hunger strike before in 2001, it wasn't really well orchestrated and it didn't come out too hot. But We were determined to try again and so on July 1st, 2011, We dropped it. And with the aid of a whole host of other revolutionary and conscious and concerned people, We were able to be successful. During the first strike, as you mentioned, there were six thousand people. CDC of course were shocked: here you got these cats locked in the short corridor and us in all these long corridors and We're still able to communicate. This is supposed to be the most maximum security prison in the country and yet We're still able to communicate and organize a strike. But We couldn't have done it without outside help from concerned supporters and it's just a beautiful thing that at that time in this day and age people had said that enough is enough.

Well, CDC came and said "Well you guys are right. We are going to start implementing those five core demands. In the meantime here's a beanie, here's a coat, We may put up a pull-up bar"—they put a couple of extra items on the canteen—"and We'll get around to those five core demands." And of course by September they hadn't gotten around to it and they had been shucking and jiving with our principal representatives, and so another hunger strike was implemented and this time We garnished the aid of twelve thousand prisoners. We doubled the amount of prisoners that participated, and thirteen prisons up and down the coast of California and several within the empire and some even around the world supported us. It was harsh because the first hunger strike, the pigs were caught unprepared,

Rally in Sacramento to support 2011 hunger strike.

and so a lot of times they didn't come and take things that We had in our cells—but by the time the second hunger strike came around, they had positioned themselves to react more swiftly and so they responded harshly because they were embarrassed by the fact that during the first one they were caught off guard.

Still, We were successful. If nothing else it showed that even in the most downtrodden situations you can still do something and that's what We proved. Still, today our five core demands have not been adequately met. The CDC has now implemented what is called a "step down program," which is just a change in language from calling us "Prison Gang" members to now calling us "Security Threat Group" members or associates, and these things will still get you life in the hole. If We ever get out, some will even say, you're a Security Threat Group member therefore you still pose a threat to the security of the institution and others and so We can't let you out. So it's a play on words. We're resisting that. We're not going for that. In fact, just the other day, in *The Rock* newsletter, put together and edited by our good comrade

The 2011 hunger strikes garnered support from coast to coast.

Ed Mead of the George Jackson Brigade, there was an article explaining how We're resisting that*—the step down program, the Security Threat Group—because it is euphemistic, it's shadowy language and what they are trying to do in effect is deem us terrorists. It's not terroristic to fight against imperialism. That's a human right to fight against oppression.

So, while We were proud to reach the amount of people that We had and to have gotten the support that We had gotten, We are by no means resting on our laurels. It's a struggle every day and even though i'm out now, if the comrades went on hunger strike today, i would go on strike right here. i would not eat right here. Because i am a member of the SHU class. i've been in prison for 25 years, 20 of those years have been in the hole, probably 22, and 3 have been in general population and so

---

* See "The Pilot Program: Security Threat Group—Identification, Interdiction, Prevention, And Management," *The Rock* vol. 2 #1 at http://www.prisonart.org/images/!Newsletter/Rock2_1.pdf

i'm a permanent SHU class prisoner. That comes with a certain amount of responsibility, consciousness and obligation.

Tookie said "moto ndani"—that's Swahili for "the fire within." As long as you have that moto ndani, that fire within, you can continue to go forward. Pelican Bay's job is to try and put that fire out and then you have people who debrief or people who lose their mind as a consequence of the pressure. We have a saying in Pelican Bay: Pelican Bay's either going to make dust or make diamonds. It's either going to pulverize you or it's going to steel you, it's going to sharpen you.

QUESTION: In your most recent writings you stress New Afrikan nationhood as opposed to a black identity. How are these different?

SANYIKA: What We are trying to do now in the New Afrikan Independence Movement, as We should have done long ago, is to get away from the usage of color to describe and denote nationalities. Because what happens is when you start saying, "i'm black, she's white, he's yellow, she's brown, she's red," you lose the identity of the people. While these colors were necessary in the '60s to get away from things like "Indian," "negro," "spic," "nigger," "wetback"—while these words were necessary to get away from those colonial words they weren't sufficient. So We see now today and We have since the '80s actually when We reformulated the whole idea of this black thing, that black is just a color, there is no continent called black. There were no black people before 1492. Black is a consequence of colonialism. Period. And so what We try to do is get out of that colonial mentality by properly describing who We are and what We want.

When We say that We are a New Afrikan people, We're saying first and foremost that We are a nation unto ourselves inside the belly of the beast, separate and distinct with our own set of contradictions. We are more than a color. We are a nationality deserving of a nation. Not only that, but when We say We're New Afrikan, We're saying We're not black, We're not amerikan. We don't want to be amerikan nor do We necessarily want to be black. We'll use it interchangeably now to people who don't really overstand but We're trying to get away from that whole race thing because there really are no races, and when you say "you're black and she's white and he's red and she's brown" you're saying there's a myriad of races on the planet and that's not the case.

The situation is this: race has been used to divide humanity, and so if We say "We're black and they're white, and she's brown, and he's yellow," We are going along with that false construct of race. When the fact of the matter is that i could have mutual relations with any female on this planet and produce a child: That means that We are of the same race. Regardless of what our nationality is, our customs, our culture, or our language or our geographical location, We are of the same race: We're humans.

What We are, however, are broken down into nationalities, with customs, cultures, linguistics and so on and so forth and that's the reality of us stressing New Afrikan nationhood. By saying you're New Afrikan, you're saying you have a right to a nationality. If you have a nationality, you consequently come from or should be trying to get a nation. Nationalities stem from nations.

The thing about racism is this: it's false and yet it's real. It's false because We know that We all can breed and procreate, if We wish. Yet it's real because it can get you killed on any street corner in this country. We know that there are racists. We know that there are white supremacists. We know that there are black supremacists—believe it or not, it is what it is. People get hung up on these colors and they start drifting off and not overstanding that what they're doing is actually promoting their own oppression because it was that division of humanity by the ruling classes of the western world that created these subjugations.

QUESTION: You are a communist at a time when the world is increasingly rocked by insurrections and rebellions but also at a time when communism is very much out of favor. Some would say that the 20th century saw communism try and fail. What do you mean by communism?

SANYIKA: i am in fact a communist. i am a New Afrikan communist. i've been a communist since 1986. i'm a proud member of a communist faction of the New Afrikan Independence Movement.

Let me say this first and foremost: the so-called prototype of communism that We've been given by Russia was no communism at all. In fact, Russia was an imperialist country since the death of Lenin, but it parlayed in drag as a communist country and the west promoted that because they knew from the beginning it was an authoritarian imperialist State and so they knew it would do nothing but make communism look bad. Now, saying that, We were grateful however, from '45 to the late '60s and a little after that, for the weapons We were able to get in the worldwide revolution from Russia. But they only gave us enough weapons so that it wouldn't actually threaten imperialism, and the studies prove that.

So in '89 or '90 there was no collapse of communism, rather it was the collapse of Soviet imperialism. You see, there's only two ways to govern any economy: socialist or capitalist. Period. There's only 2 ways. People may say that communism is out of favor or has failed, but there is no country that has ever reached communism. China since '79, actually since the death of Mao Tse Tung in '76, has been a State capitalist government. There

is no communism there, of course, it's just State crony capitalism. There's been no country that has ever reached that stage.
Communism is the highest form of socialism. It's the dissolu-
tion of all classes. No country, not even the great Cuba today, has
reached that stage.

So there is no communism, there's just communists, believe
it or not, because no one has reached that stage yet. Capitalism,
however has had such a long run and it feeds into such narcis-
sistic and egotistical human traits that it has longevity and, i got
to say it, capitalism is revolutionary. It continually changes, it
adapts, it moves, it fosters the image of well-being—but that's
just the outer shell.

i'm a communist in the sense that i believe in the equal
distribution of wealth and privilege. i believe in equality, i believe
in the dictatorship of the proletariat. i'm a working-class person,
whether i got a job or not, i have a working-class mentality. That
means that i'm down with those who toil, with those who labor.
And not just the laborers, but students. i'm down with the masses, those who have the foot of the State on their neck and are
having their labor exploited. i'm a communist because i believe in
the community. i believe that the community is more important
than the individual. i'm a communist because i believe in a socialist system. i am anti-capitalist, and i'm not just anti-capitalist but
i'm pro-socialist. So to me to be a communist is to be in the resistance, is to be anti that which has been killing humanity since it
evolved from feudalism as a consequence of colonialism.

QUESTION: You've written about capitalism and about colonialism. Some of your writings also deal with patriarchy, homophobia and transphobia. How do all of these things fit together?

SANYIKA: You know, that's a good question. People are becoming little oppressors unto themselves as a consequence of the oppression that has since 1619 been stationed over our heads here. As a consequence of living so close to the seat of empire, so close to the beast, We begin to take on the traits of the beast and then We'll cloak it in some super-duper black shit, for instance as if homosexuality didn't exist before the Arabs and the Europeans came to Afrika—as if they brought that.

   i heard one dude say it's a consequence of some mental—wait, i've gotta say this: Because this idiot, and that's what he is, he's an idiot, this dude (and i won't say his name because i want to talk to him personally first), this idiot is one of those super-duper black dudes and what he does is he goes around with this super-duper black shit and he is trying to convince our people first and foremost that the white man is the devil. He's still on that crap even though We got Rock Bottom Obama up there. But, in one instance he's saying that the white man is the devil and then in the next instance to prove his point that homosexuality is a mental disease he quotes the same white man he calls the devil in his mental health writings. So that's a contradiction unto itself.

   The fact of the matter is, as revolutionaries, as oppressed people, We don't have the luxury of excluding any other oppressed person from struggling or living. Who are We to say that as a consequence of who you sleep with or who you are attracted to that you don't deserve freedom, that you're abnormal? That's the same stuff they used to say about us as a consequence of our skin being darker or our noses being broader or our hair being curlier or our phalluses being bigger or whatever. As a consequence of the slightest difference the system would exclude us and use that, à la Willie Lynch letter, to oppress us... and yet here We come in master's tracks, oppressing as little oppressors other oppressed people.

Martin Luther King said, "Don't judge someone by the color of their skin, but the content of their character." The same applies when it comes to this whole gender thing. Gender is just as made up as race—it's real and yet it's not real. i'll be damned if i exclude somebody from helping the rest of us get free or themselves getting free as a consequence of who they sleep with, what they wear, what color their hair is... The issue is: are you down with armed struggle? Are you honest? Are you responsible? What can you contribute to the struggle? Are you with us or are you against us? That's the only thing We need to know.

Gay Liberation Front members supporting the Black Panther Party (left, late 1960s), and poster for demonstration supporting the New Jersey 4, New Afrikan lesbians jailed for defending themselves against street harassment in 2006.

i think as revolutionaries We need to lead the struggle on issues of homophobia, transphobia, against racism with this whole black black thing or white white thing. What made the revolutionaries of the '60s and '70s so potent was that their theory was on the cutting edge of where We needed to go. It was so critical, it was so sharp that it was almost insane. And you see that that's the beauty of correct theory: it's so far ahead that it's looked at as abnormal. So when We come out and say We recruit gays, lesbians, transgendered people, bisexuals, We recruit anybody that's oppressed, the super-duper black black people look at us like "there they go!" (We heard one idiot say, "The gay movement has hijacked the civil rights movement"—civil rights ain't a black thing! Civil rights is a neo-colonial thing: civil rights means you're trying to be a citizen of the oppressor nation!)

My point is: it's not about who you sleep with, when you sleep with them, what you wear when you sleep with them, what you do in the comfort of your own bedroom, or wherever. It's about "are you down with us or not?" That's the issue and that's the only issue our movement should have with anybody. You know, i'm not concerned what color your complexion is, i'm not concerned about how long your hair is, i'm not concerned if you got on two shoes or one or high heels or flats. i'm concerned about can you do the job given to you adequately, responsibly? Can you respond to the people's needs? Can you contribute to us getting free?

The beast already recognizes this. The beast already opened up its ranks. The beast said, "Don't ask. Don't tell," and then they demolished that. So if the reactionaries are getting ahead of the revolutionaries, what does that say about the revolutionaries? So yeah, our thing is that We get down with anybody that's oppressed. Anybody that wants to fight is welcome to join the revolution.

QUESTION: In August 2012 you were finally released from prison. What is it like being on the outside after so many years in isolation? What are your conditions on the outside?

SANYIKA: Pelican Bay, over the years since '89, has taken its toll on me. And i didn't really recognize it until this time when i got out, that i picked up a few OCDs—"Obsessive Compulsive Disorders." i'm meticulous about cleaning. i have anxiety issues. i can't sleep a lot of times throughout the week; i sleep maybe two days in a row good, and the other five days, they're up and down erratic sleeping patterns. i respond to loud sounds. i have a fear of crowds. Fast moving objects, bright colors tend to disorientate me. And here it is now, January 1st, and i'm just now starting to get acclimated to spaces, wide open spaces.

i think the older i get, the more sensitive i become, and the sensitivity is derived from a consequence of being isolated. And so the slightest touch, the slightest sound, the slightest smell, it stimulates me to a point where i'm overstimulated and i become disoriented. It's hard to write, it's hard to read, to concentrate.

You see, these are the things We say about Pelican Bay being a torture chamber, and i've been out. i've never done longer than 5 years—this is the longest i've ever done which is 5 years and 5 months. But this is my third 5 year term, where actually i've had 7 years and done 5 each time, it's three times—and all in the hole and then with violations to boot. But just think about the prisoner who hasn't been out since '89, who's just been in that one box since '89 and has not just an indeterminate but a life term. Think about him or her in that situation.

My conditions of parole, of course, are all political. i was kicked out of Los Angeles county and dropped off in San Diego. i got an ankle bracelet on, a GPS, they can see everywhere i go. i got forty four special conditions of parole: things as small as i can't hitchhike, i can't have a mask on Halloween, i can't have surveillance equipment. It's a myriad of forty four special conditions. Let me say this: when i was a criminal, i went to prison two times for shooting several people. Each time i got out for shooting several people, i had four conditions: no guns, no drugs, no gangs, can't travel 50 miles from my parole agent. This time a carjacking, a piece of steel that was deprived from an idiot: forty four special conditions. Aside from the four i already have, so actually it's forty eight, an ankle bracelet and kicked out of the county of Los Angeles. L.A. was fine when i was shooting people, L.A. was fine when i was Monster Kody, L.A. was fine when i was selling drugs, using drugs. That was all good with L.A.. But when you become a revolutionary, you become a threat—and not to the institutional security of a prison but to the institution of capitalism. And that's what's really cracking. So it is what it is: i think that if they let me out of Pelican Bay and didn't do nothing, i'd have been doing something wrong. So it's the dialectical relationship, it is what it is.

It hasn't slowed me down one bit. At the same time, i'm cautious. i'm respectful. i'm courteous. i'm hopeful. i'm an optimist. i get up every morning thinking that today's going to be better than yesterday was. You know, why get up if you don't think that? i think that We are on the right side of social development. i think that if We survive, We can win. i think that one of our biggest problems is that We self-defeat—We think We can't, when obviously the beast knows that We can otherwise why would they be doing us like this? If they didn't have faith in us—and they tend to have more faith in us than We have in ourselves sometimes—if they didn't have faith in us to get free, then why would they oppress us such?

Pelican Bay State Prison
THE EFFECTS OF STARVATION

Prolonged starvation can result in serious harm to a person's body and mind. When a person's food intake falls far below the body's daily needs, a complex series of defensive changes are set in motion by the body in an effort to protect itself. These changes go far beyond a simple loss of weight and a very thin appearance. If these defensive changes are needed for too long, they become a form of disease that can proceed to unstoppable damage to your health and can result in death. There is a point where starting to eat and full medical care cannot stop or reverse the continued decline in health.

When there is a loss of food intake, the body draws on itself to maintain blood glucose, its main fuel. It is untrue the body will only use fat first. With no protein intake, muscle tissue is also used from the beginning. Each pound of fat the body burns needs a pound of protein to be burned with it. Beyond the production of energy, a certain amount of protein is needed for the functioning of the body's chemistry. When fat stores are exhausted, the body will have only the destruction of muscle and organ tissue to produce energy; all organs are involved. Therefore, any existing disease in an organ can be especially dangerous. You will receive a risk assessments based on your health records to determine if you have increased risks associated with your pre-existing disease. The heart is an organ that is constantly working is therefore especially at risk. Heart failure and sudden disturbance of the heart beat are the leading cause of death in fasting. Often the damage to the heart is lasting after a fast and full weight recovery. The skin becomes thin, dry, inelastic, pale and cold, and bones protrude. A patchy brown pigmentation may occur. Hair becomes dry and sparse and falls out easily. Diarrhea may occur and hasten the wasting process. When the brain does not have enough glucose to allow thinking, apathy and irritability occur followed by coma and death.

170

Proteins are needed for the maintenance of the body's chemistry and are especially important. When the body's proteins have been depleted to approximately one-half of their normal levels, eating will not help because there is no ability to absorb and process food. Full medical intervention will not reverse the affects, which are likely to lead to death.

Other negative changes in the chemistry of the body also occur. Vitamin deficiencies occur, particularly the Vitamin B group and Vitamin C and further weaken the body. Resistance to disease and infections decreases making the body vulnerable to other illnesses. Calcium is removed from the bones to be used for the body's needs. The bones become permanently weaker and more subject to painful breakage, and do not regain calcium later. Kidney stones are also very common with fasting.

With the loss of fluids, wasting, protein loss, and vitamin deficiencies organ function declines markedly. The kidneys and liver are unable to process chemicals including your medications. As a precaution from overdosing on medications, all non-essential medications will be discontinued. All other drugs will be carefully evaluated and most likely reduced in dose.

You may refuse to eat solid food, drink fluids, or both. While much of the same affects occur with fluid refusal; the time considerations are much more rapid. The refusal to drink fluids is far more serious to the point that death occurs within a week. Even a short period of no fluids can result in kidney damage which may be permanent.

I understand that my refusal to eat or drink can bring about the above adverse and possibly deadly effects (as well as others) on my body and my well being.

Political Prisoner!

Page 1 of

Memoranc.

Date : September 27, 2011

To : All CDCR Inmates

Subject: INMATE PROGRAMMING EXPECTATIONS RELATIVE TO HUNGER STRIKES

Information has been received that a number of inmates have engaged in behavior consistent with initiating a demonstration/hunger strike event. The Department will not condone organized inmate disturbances. Participation in mass disturbances, such as hunger strikes or work stoppage will result in the Department taking the following action:

- Inmates participating will receive disciplinary action in accordance with the California Code of Regulations.
- Inmates identified as leading the disturbance will be subject to removal from general population and placed in an Administrative Segregation Unit.
- In the event of a mass hunger strike, additional measures may be taken to more effectively monitor and manage the participating inmates' involvement and their food/nutrition intake, including the possible removal of canteen items from participating inmates.

All inmates are encouraged to continue with positive programming and to not participate in this or any other identified mass strike/disturbance. These types of disturbances impact inmate programming and day-to-day prison operations for the entire population. While every effort will be made to continue normal programming for nonparticipating inmates, a large scale disturbance of this type will unavoidably impact operations. The Department will notify inmates and families when and if normal programming is impacted.

SCOTT KERNAN
Undersecretary (A), Operations

cc: Terri McDonald
George J. Giurbino
R. J. Subia
Kelly Harrington
Tony Chaus
Wardens

DEPARTMENT OF CORRECTIONS
CDC 128B (Rev. 4/74

Number: D-07829   **Name: SCOTT**

Housing: C7-112L

The California Code of Regulations, Title 15, identifies that leading and/or participation in a strike, disturbance or work stoppage is a violation of the Director's Rules. On or about July 1, 2011 you were identified as having participated in a state wide hunger strike event along with in excess of 6000 other CDCR inmates in support of perceived overly harsh SHU Housing issues originating from within the Security Housing Unit at Pelican Bay State Prison. This activity created a non-violent significant disruption to institutional Health Care Services and Department of Corrections programming and operations throughout the State, which included Pelican Bay State Prison, where you were assigned during your participation in this event. Your behavior and actions were out of compliance with the Director's Rules, and this documentation is intended to record your actions; and advise that progressive discipline will be taken in the future for any reoccurrence of this type of behavior.

J. Welch
CORRECTIONAL OFFICER

ORIG: C-FILE
cc: AWC
    INMATE
    PROGRAM
    CCI
    UNIT (2)

INFORMATIONAL CHRONO

DATE: 08/02/11

Inst: PBSP

Front view of a cell in Pelican Bay SHU's notorious "short corridor." The locked tray slot is where food trays, mail, etc. are delivered.
The cell shown in the following photographs belonged to prisoner representative Todd Ashker.

View from approximately one step inside cell door area, showing cement slab bunks in a PB-SHU cell on D-Corridor. Back concrete wall along bunks is not insulated—6" of cold concrete separates cell from the outside and cells are like meat locker ice boxes in winter; as such prisoners often sleep on the floor.

View of front of cell from inside cell. The home made shelf holding Ashker's cosmetics (shampoo, soap, lotion, toothpaste) was destroyed by prison staff in June 2011.

View of sink, toilet, desk area with TV which this prisoner has had since 1992; and cement stool. Bags are canteen that had just been received; most of which are nearly empty.

Floor area standing just inside cell, rough concrete floor.

Who Are You?

We are the ones who refused to be captured in Afrika without a fight, who staged daring raids on enemy supply lines and brought our nationals back to freedom. We are the ones who made longer, sharper spears, thicker shields and turned our backs on collaborating kings.

We are the ones who, on the high seas en route to the "New World," brought new forms of combat to bear on our oppressors. We are the ones who couldn't be broken, who kept our languages in circulation, our spirits alive and our minds free of foreign gods and hostile demons. We are those who, on a move, became Maroons, who settled the Geechi Islands, fought alongside the indigenous nations, until we, too, became indigenous.

We are the ones who, in the midst of the first Two Thousand Seasons (a thousand dry, a thousand wet), birthed new ideas of national existence and national continuity.

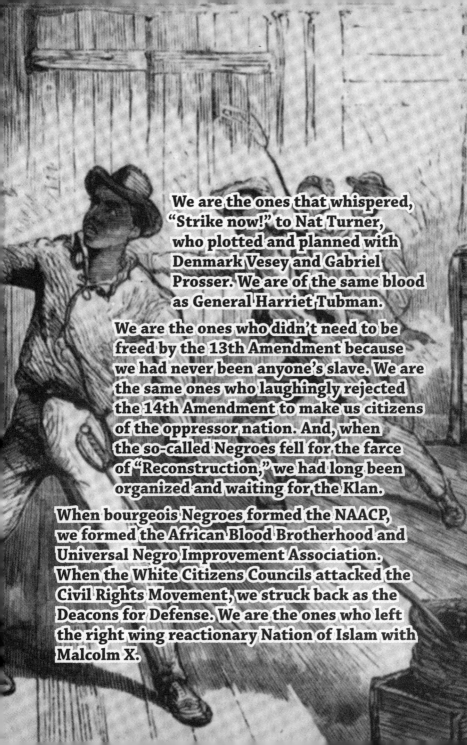

We are the ones that whispered, "Strike now!" to Nat Turner, who plotted and planned with Denmark Vesey and Gabriel Prosser. We are of the same blood as General Harriet Tubman.

We are the ones who didn't need to be freed by the 13th Amendment because we had never been anyone's slave. We are the same ones who laughingly rejected the 14th Amendment to make us citizens of the oppressor nation. And, when the so-called Negroes fell for the farce of "Reconstruction," we had long been organized and waiting for the Klan.

When bourgeois Negroes formed the NAACP, we formed the African Blood Brotherhood and Universal Negro Improvement Association. When the White Citizens Councils attacked the Civil Rights Movement, we struck back as the Deacons for Defense. We are the ones who left the right wing reactionary Nation of Islam with Malcolm X.

We are the ones who organized the ghettos, from California to Philly, as the Revolutionary Action Movement. We were in Monroe with Robert and Mabel Williams. We sat at the feet of Queen Mother Moore, Ella Baker and Dara Abubakari. We are the ones who adopted the attacking Black Panther as our symbol, those who stared down pigs, created Black Student Unions and fed free breakfast to children. We sharpened the contradiction.

We are the ones who, realizing the neo-colonial nature of the term "Negro," changed our national identity to Black. When that term, too, had been co-opted by opportunists and counter revolutionaries, we are the ones who converged on Detroit 500 deep and brought into existence the New Afrikan national identity. We are the ones who said Louisiana, Alabama, Mississippi, Georgia and South Carolina is the National Territory.

We are the ones who breathed life into the Black Liberation Army, who proceeded to combat our historical enemies from coast to coast and all areas in between. We were on the roof in New Orleans with Mark Essex, in South Central L.A. with Geronimo ji Jaga, in El-Malik at the Capitol with the RNA-11. We are the ones who were in Chicago with Santa Bear and Spurgeon Jake Winters; in Attica with L.D. and Sam Melville. We were in Soledad with George, Fleeta and John; in the Marin County Courthouse with Jonathan, William, James and Ruchell. We are the ones who were with George, Hugo and Bato in San Quentin.

We are the ones from the George L. Jackson Assault Squad of the BLA in San Francisco. We are the ones in both Olugbala and Amistad Collectives of the BLA. And that was us in the Five Percenter-BLA units, too. We invaded the tombs to free our comrades and went underwater to assault Riker's Island as well. We are the ones who made Nicky Barnes run to the Italian mob for protection.

We are the ones who were in support
of the United Freedom Front, the
May 19th Communist Organization,
the George Jackson Brigade, the
Sam Melville-Jonathan Jackson Unit,
and the Prairie Fire/John Brown
Anti-Klan Committee. We are the
ones who introduced Comrade-Sista
Assata Shakur to Fidel and Raul. We
hooked Robert Williams up with Mao
and Chou En Lai.

We are the ones who defended
the people in a raging gun battle
against pigs at Aretha Franklin's
father's church in Detroit. We are
the ones who brought you Kuwasi
Balagoon, Dr. Mutulu Shakur,
Nehanda Abiodun, Fulani Sunni
Ali, Safiya Bukhari, Yassmyn Fula,
Afeni Shakur, Sundiata Acoli, Maliki
Shakur Latine, Sekou Odinga, Jalil
Muntaqim, Herman Bell and all the
other stalwart standard bearers of
liberation.

We are the ones
who speak truth to
power, who practice
our theories, who
are the messages we
bring. We are the ones
in the Provisional
Government Republic
of New Afrika, People's
Center Council, The
People's Revolutionary
Leadership Council,
New Afrikan People's
Organization, New
Afrikan Panthers, New
Afrikan Scouts, Spear
and Shield Collective,
Malcolm X Grassroots
Movement, August
Third Collective, New
Afrikan Security
Forces, Revolutionary
Armed Task Force,
New Afrikan People's
Liberation Army and
New Afrikan Women
for Self-Determination.
And We'll be in many
more to come.

We are the ones who support Puerto Rican Independence, the Mexicano/Chicano Movement, the American Indian Movement and all other revolutionary struggles for freedom against capitalist imperialism. We are those who stand firm against patriarchy, heterosexualism and liberalism. We are those that study Butch Lee, J. Sakai, Owusu Yaki Yakubu, Chokwe Lumumba, Makungu Akinyela, Che, Cabral, Fanon and Dr. John Henrik Clarke. We are the ones who know that "revolution without women ain't happenin'"!

We are the ones the enemy calls, "criminals," "terrorists," "gangs," "militants," "leftists," "separatists," "radicals," "feminists," "worst of the worst," "America's Most Wanted" and enemy combatants. Whatever.

We call ourselves Humans. We are New Afrikan revolutionaries. Those who weren't afraid.

Who are you?
Free the Land!

Appendices

Appendix I

Five Core Demands of the 2011 California Prisoners Hungerstrike[*]

1. End Group Punishment & Administrative Abuse—This is in response to Pelican Bay State Prison's application of "group punishment" as a means to address individual inmates rule violations. This includes the administration's abusive, pretextual use of "safety and concern" to justify what are unnecessary punitive acts. This policy has been applied in the context of justifying indefinite SHU status, and progressively restricting our programming and privileges.

2. Abolish the Debriefing Policy, and Modify Active/Inactive Gang Status Criteria—

  → Perceived gang membership is one of the leading reasons for placement in solitary confinement.
  → The practice of "debriefing," or offering up information about fellow prisoners particularly regarding gang status, is often demanded in return for better food or release from the SHU. Debriefing puts the safety of prisoners and their families at risk, because they are then viewed as "snitches."

---

* These demands were issued on April 3, 2011, by Todd Ashker, Arturo Castellanos, Sitawa N. Jamaa (s/n R.N. Dewberry), George Franco, Antonio Guillen, Lewis Powell, Paul Redd, Alfred Sandoval, Danny Troxell, James Williamson and Ronnie Yandell, on behalf of all other similarly situated prisoners.

→ The validation procedure used by the California Department of Corrections and Rehabilitation (CDCR) employs such criteria as tattoos, readings materials, and associations with other prisoners (which can amount to as little as greeting) to identify gang members.

→ Many prisoners report that they are validated as gang members with evidence that is clearly false or using procedures that do not follow the *Castillo v. Alameida* settlement which restricted the use of photographs to prove association.

3. Comply with the U.S. Commission on Safety and Abuse in America's Prisons 2006 Recommendations Regarding an End to Long-Term Solitary Confinement—CDCR shall implement the findings and recommendations of the U.S. Commission on Safety and Abuse in America's Prisons final 2006 report regarding CDCR SHU facilities as follows:

→ End Conditions of Isolation (p. 14)

→ Ensure that prisoners in SHU and Ad-Seg (Administrative Segregation) have regular meaningful contact and freedom from extreme physical deprivations that are known to cause lasting harm. (pp. 52-57)

→ Make Segregation a Last Resort (p. 14).

→ Create a more productive form of confinement in the areas of allowing inmates in SHU and Ad-Seg the opportunity to engage in meaningful self-help treatment, work, education, religious, and other productive activities relating to having a sense of being a part of the community.

→ End Long-Term Solitary Confinement. Release inmates to general prison population who have been
warehoused indefinitely in SHU for the last 10 to 40
years (and counting).
→ Provide SHU Inmates Immediate Meaningful Access
to: *(i)* adequate natural sunlight; *(ii)* quality health
care and treatment, including the mandate of trans-
ferring all PBSP-SHU inmates with chronic health
care problems to the New Folsom Medical SHU
facility.

4.   Provide Adequate and Nutritious Food—cease the practice
of denying adequate food, and provide a wholesome nutritional
meals including special diet meals, and allow inmates to purchase
additional vitamin supplements.

→ PBSP staff must cease their use of food as a tool to
punish SHU inmates.
→ Provide a sergeant/lieutenant to independently observe the serving of each meal, and ensure each tray
has the complete issue of food on it.
→ Feed the inmates whose job it is to serve SHU meals
with meals that are separate from the pans of food
sent from kitchen for SHU meals.

5.   Expand and Provide Constructive Programming and
Privileges for Indefinite SHU Status Inmates. Examples include:

→ Expand visiting regarding amount of time and add-
ing one day per week.
→ Allow one photo per year.

→ Allow a weekly phone call.

→ Allow Two (2) annual packages per year. A 30 lb. package based on "item" weight and not packaging and box weight.

→ Expand canteen and package items allowed. Allow us to have the items in their original packaging [the cost for cosmetics, stationary, envelopes, should not count towards the max draw limit]

→ More TV channels.

→ Allow TV/Radio combinations, or TV and small battery operated radio

→ Allow Hobby Craft Items—art paper, colored pens, small pieces of colored pencils, watercolors, chalk, etc.

→ Allow sweat suits and watch caps.

→ Allow wall calendars.

→ Install pull-up/dip bars on SHU yards.

→ Allow correspondence courses that require proctored exams.

Appendix 2
Counterinsurgency Memos

The following eleven pages consist of counterinsurgency memos issued regarding Sanyika Shakur, in which he was "validated" by the political police of the Calfornia Department of Corrections and Rehabilitation (CDCR). As explained on page 154:

> In 1989, in September, i was given my final point: it takes three points to be given what's called indeterminate or to be validated. So i got my third point in 1989: they said i had written a letter with revolutionary overtones. That landed me in Ad-Seg in Soledad. When i got to Ad-Seg, they had a situation, a group of people there called CAC, Criminal Activities Coordinator, which is IGI (Institutional Gang Investigations). They went through their investigation and they said in 1988 i had been observed exercising in military fashion with known revolutionaries in Folsom Prison, and then in 1987 they said while in San Quentin i had received some writings by Comrade George Jackson that someone had sent me through the mail. i never got it, they intercepted it; they never told me they had intercepted it, nor did they tell me they had taken pictures of me and these revolutionaries exercising in Folsom in '88. Well in '89 when i came back they had started the new Pelican Bay validation program, and i already had two points. So when they said i had written a letter with revolutionary overtones in '89, that was my third and final point. That in effect gave me life in the hole.

NAME and NUMBER KODY,SCOTT D-07829 AKA MONSTER/CODY-SANYIKA LB-332

CAC investigation has been conducted to determine inmate Scott's gang status.Particular,
attention is directed to a Confidential dated 8-31-88,Folsom State Prison outlining exercises
and meetings conducted by known Black Guerilla Family Members and Associates.Inmate Scott was a
participant of both.On 9-17-89,inmate Scott was placed on CTO status per CTF-North Facality
staff pending investigation for attempting to mail letters with BGF overtones.Inmate Scott is a
member of the,"Eight Tray Crips"conviction is gang related.Based on inmate Scott's Confidential
File inmate Scott is being documented as a Black Guerilla Family Associate.Inmate Benson D-63433
mentioned in the 8-11-88 Confidential is considered to be a BGF General.Inmate Scott was assessed
SHU term in 1985 for"Conspiracy to Assault Staff".CDC 812/812-A were updated.

This document meets the
Original:Central File validation requirements
cc:P.A.   established in CCR Title
        CC-II   15 Section 3378
        CC-I
        C&PR

                                    Lt. J. Crowder,CAC
                                    CAC CTF Complex

DATE 9-18-89   Criminal Activities Coordinator Investigations CTF   GENERAL CHRONO

STATE OF CALIFORNIA
CDC 1030 (12/86)

DEPARTMENT OF CORRECTIONS

CONFIDENTIAL INFORMATION DISCLOSURE FORM

INMATE NUMBER: _D07829_ INMATE NAME: _Scott, Kony_

1) Use of Confidential Information.

Information received from a confidential source(s) has been considered in the:

a) CDC-115, Disciplinary Report dated _____ submitted by

_____
STAFF NAME, TITLE

b) CDC-114-D, Order and Hearing for Placement in Segregated Housing dated _12/14/98_

2) Reliability of Source.

The identity of the source(s) cannot be disclosed without endangering the source(s) or the security of the institution.

This information is considered reliable because:

a) ☐ This source has previously provided confidential information which has proven to be true.

b) ☐ This source participated in and successfully completed a Polygraph examination.

c) ☐ More than one source independently provided the same information.

d) ☐ This source indicated through its firsthand or eyewitness activity at the time of providing the information

c) more than one source independently provided the same information.

d) ☐ This source incriminated himself/herself in a criminal activity at the time of providing the information.

e) ☐ Part of the information provided by the source(s) has already proven to be true.

f) ☒ Other (EXPLAIN) THE INFORMATION IF KNOWN BY OTHER INMATES, WOULD ENDANGER THE SAFETY OF INMATES AND THE SAFETY AND SECURITY OF THE INSTITUTION.

3) Disclosure of information received.

The information received indicated the following: A CONFIDENTIAL MEMORANDUM DATED 12/11/86, AN ENVELOPE ADDRESSED TO SCOTT, CONTAINED BLACK RADICAL INFORMATION ENTITLED "THE NEW BLACK COMMUNIST", AND ALSO INSIDE THE ENVELOPE INCLUDED WRITINGS FROM INMATE JACKSON, GEORGE, A63837.

_____

(if additional space needed, attach another sheet.)

4) Type and current location of documentation, (for example: CDC-128-B of 6-15-86 in the confidential material folder). A CONFIDENTIAL MEMORANDUM DATED 12/11/86, AUTHORED BY M.K. FITTS LOCATED IN SCOTTS CENTRAL FILE, CONFIDENTIAL SECTION.

_____   3-19-99

STATE OF CALIFORNIA

CDC 128-B-2 (4/07)

DEPARTMENT OF CORRECTIONS AND REHABILITATION

INMATE'S NAME: SCOTT, KODY　　　　　　　　　**CDCR NUMBER: D07829**

On September 2, 1989, a validation package was received from Institution Gang Investigator, J. Crowder at CTF. On August 31, 1995, a CDCR 128B2 regarding Subject was issued identifying Subject as an active Black Guerrilla Family associate.

On March 10, 1999, a CDCR 128B2 was issued updating Kody's status as an active Black Guerrilla Family associate.

On September 15, 2008, a gang validation package regarding subject was received from Institution Gang Investigator R. Rice at PBSP.

This CDC-128B2 reflects additional information which updates Subject's status.

The following items meet the validation requirements:　　　　　　　**TOTAL NUMBER OF ITEMS SUBMITTED FOR REVIEW: (3)**

1. CDCR 128B dated September 4, 2008 (Correspondence/Written Material)
2. CDCR 128B dated September 3, 2008 (Correspondence/Written Material) Support to CDCR 128B dated 9/3/08

TOTAL NUMBER ITEMS WHICH MEET VALIDATION REQUIREMENTS: (2)

The following items do not meet the validation requirements and were/shall not be used as a basis for validation:

1. Confidential Memorandum dated January 24, 2008 (Informant/Staff Information) Support information not included.

TOTAL NUMBER OF ITEMS WHICH DO NOT MEET VALIDATION REQUIREMENTS: (1)

TOTAL NUMBER OF ITEMS WHICH DO NOT MEET VALIDATION REQUIREMENTS: (1)

ACTION OF REVIEWER

Pursuant to the validation requirements established in 15 CCR Section 3378, SCOTT, KODY is:

☒ VALIDATED   ☐ REJECTED

as an associate of the BLACK GUERRILLA FAMILY prison gang.

CHAIRPERSON
PRINTED NAME

REVIEWER
T.L. Rosencrans
PRINTED NAME

MEMBER
Scott S Kissel
PRINTED NAME

ACTIVE/INACTIVE REVIEW

August 27, 2014

_____
ELIGIBILITY DATE

DISTRIBUTION:
Original – Central File
Copy – Classification & Parole Representative/Parole Administrator I
Copy – Institutional Gang Investigator/Regional Gang Coordinator
Copy – Office of Correctional Safety – Special Service Unit
Copy – Inmate/Parolee 12-5-08 by KGott cct

DATE: 10/24/08   SSU GANG VALIDATION/REJECTION REVIEW   GENERAL CHRONO

NAME: SCOTT, Kody   *CDC #* D-07829

On August 13, 2008, an investigation was initiated by Institutional Gang Investigations Unit (IGI) in reference to validated Black Guerrilla Family (BGF) associate, Kody SCOTT, D-07829, aka "Monster/Dreamer/Sanyika Shakur," per the California Code of Regulations (CCR), Section 3378 (e), regarding his current gang status. SCOTT was validated as an associate of the BGF prison gang based upon a gang validation package submitted by Institution Gang Investigator F.B. Haws at California Correctional Institution (CCI) on March 4, 1999. The source items used to validate SCOTT are all over six (6) years old. Therefore, per CCR, Title 15, Section 3378 (e), SCOTT meets the criteria for an Active/Inactive Status Review. During this current investigation the following areas were reviewed relevant to BGF prison gang activity:

(Central File) The Central File of SCOTT revealed the following documented gang activity:

1. **Source Document (Informant/Staff Information)** Confidential Memorandum, dated January 24, 2008, documented is the fact that on January 24, 2008, at San Quentin State Prison, a cell search was conducted on two Blood Line affiliates. During the course of the search, an address book was confiscated from each of the inmates. A roster within the two address books contained identical names and CDC numbers, throughout the address books, all of which were BGF members or associates. On the roster was SCOTT's name and CDC identification number. With SCOTT's name included in the roster, it is reasonable to believe he is recognized by the BGF as active and in good standings with the BGF prison gang. To be in "good standings," the individual is functioning under the gang's policies, procedures, rules and guidelines. This documentation meets the criteria for gang involvement as prescribed in California Code of Regulations CCR, Title 15, Section 3378 (c)(8) (H)(E), Informant/Staff Information.

(**Property Search**) A property search was conducted by the IGI resulting in no documented gang activity.

On September 3, 2008, new information was obtained regarding the ongoing gang status of inmate SCOTT. The Control Booth officer in the housing unit where SCOTT resides contacted and advised me that he had intercepted and photocopied two letters that SCOTT was attempting to send out. He also advised me that he had written a CDC 128-B dated September 3, 2008, on an outgoing letter dated August 28, 2008, but the second letter had not yet been documented. Copies of both the letters were relinquished to me to complete the investigation into continued gang activity.

2. **Source Document (Written Material)** A CDC 128-B dated September 3, 2008, authored by Correctional Officer M. Pitts-Campbell, documents the fact that an outgoing letter was intercepted by staff at Pelican Bay State Prison, authored by inmate SCOTT. On the letter above the salutations was the date "Black August 28, 2008. "Black August" was initiated by members of the BGF to commemorate all of the fallen members that had died in the month of August. These members include George Jackson (co-founder of the BGF), Jeffery Gaulden (Commander of the BGF after the death of Jackson), William Christmas, James McClain, and Jonathan Jackson (all three killed in August during an attempted escape at the Marin County Courthouse in 1970). This documentation meets the criteria for gang involvement as prescribed in California Code of Regulations CCR, Title 15, Section 3378 (c)(8) (C), Written Material.

3. **Supporting Document (Written Material)** A CDC 128-B dated September 4, 2008, documents the fact that an outgoing letter was intercepted by staff at Pelican Bay State Prison, authored by inmate SCOTT. The outgoing letter was dated August 27, 2008, addressed to Ms. Cassandra B., 20552 Lee Road, Perris, California, 92570. At the top of the letter, SCOTT writes Black August 27, 2008, and signs the last page "Sanyika."

"Black August" or the Black August movement is a concept which was established by the BGF to commemorate all of their fallen comrades. The BGF picked the month of August due to the fact that several members and associates of the BGF had been killed in the month of August. These members include George Jackson (co-founder of the BGF, killed during an attempted escape from San Quentin State Prison on August 21, 1971,) Jeffery Gaulden (Commander of the BGF after the death of Jackson, killed during a football game at San Quentin State Prison on August 1, 1978), William Christmas, James McClain, and Jonathan Jackson (all three killed on August 7, 1970, during an attempted escape at the Marin County Courthouse,) death of Alvin Miller, Cleveland Edwards, and W. L. Nolan, who were shot and killed by correctional staff during an incident with the Aryan Brotherhood, (this incident actually took place on January 13, 1970, but BGF utilize the date of August 13, 1970, to commemorate their death.) The BGF also utilize other occurrences not directly involving the BGF, but occurred in the moth of August. This includes the Watts Riots in August 1965, arrival of the first black slaves in the 13 colonies in August 1619, Underground Railroad August 1850, the birth of Marcus Garvey August 17, 1887, and birth of Black Panther Fred Hampton on August 30, 1948.

By SCOTT utilizing the Black August concept to pay tribute and homage to highly-regarded BGF gang members who died for the "advancement," shows that SCOTT is still actively participating in the ideology of the BGF gang.

This document supports source item #2.

This documentation meets the criteria for gang involvement as prescribed in CCR, Title 15, Section 3378 (c) (8) (C), Written Material.

(Archives) SCOTT is still serving under his original CDCR number, and does not have an archive file.

(WSIN) No additional information was provided by this source.

(Local Law Enforcement) Local law enforcement was not contacted as SCOTT has been in CDCR custody for the last six years.

(Paroles/Leads) Paroles were not contacted as SCOTT has been in CDCR custody for the last six years.

(Cal Gangs) No additional information was provided by this source.

(SSU/OCS) No additional information was provided by this source.

On September 3, 2008, SCOTT was cooperative with the taking of photographs for the update of his Active/Inactive Review. SCOTT has a TABE score of 9.9 and, therefore, does not require, nor did he request, staff assistance. SCOTT is not a participant in the Mental Health Delivery System.

2

On September 3, 2008, SCOTT was issued a copy of the CDC 1030, Confidential Information Disclosure Form used in the update, as well one (1) itemized pre-printed page for his response. SCOTT was advised that the IGI would interview him after 24 hours regarding the information used in the update. SCOTT was informed that during the interview, he would have the opportunity to present his response regarding the information used.

On September 5, 2008, due to new information obtained on September 3, 3008, specifically, the CDC 128-B dated September 3, 2008, and the CDC 128-B dated September 4, 2008, SCOTT was reissued a new copy of the CDC 1030 Confidential Information Disclosure Form and non confidential documents used in the update. Two (2) itemized pre-printed pages listing the items used in the review was also given to SCOTT on September 5, 2008, addressing the confidential and nonconfidential documents used in the update. SCOTT was advised that he was entitled to an additional 24 hours of preparation time for the interview, and at that time, IGI would interview him regarding the information used in the update. SCOTT was informed that during the interview, he would have the opportunity to present his response regarding the information used.

On September 8, 2008, SCOTT was interviewed relative to the documents used in the review. SCOTT submitted no response on the pre-printed itemized pages I had supplied him for his response and had no further statements to make regarding the review process, and only wanted to know why IGI had stopped his mail. Based on the information obtained during this investigation it is the opinion of this investigator the submission of this validation is warranted.

Pursuant to the CCR, Title 15, Section 3378 (c), the IGI recommends that the gang status of **Kody SCOTT, D-07829**, aka **"Monster/Dreamer/Sanyika Shakur"** remain **unchanged** as **an associate of the Black Guerrilla Family (BGF) prison gang.** This information will be forwarded to the Office of Correctional Safety to update SCOTT's gang status. At SCOTT's request, he will be eligible for an Inactive Gang Status Review after August 2014. This date is based upon information contained in SCOTT Central File, specifically the CDC 128-B dated September 4, 2008, evidencing BGF gang activity in August of 2008.

S. BURRIS
Correctional Officer
Institutional Gang Investigations
Pelican Bay State Prison

R. RICE
Correctional Lientenant
Institutional Gang Investigations
Pelican Bay State Prison

DATE: *September 8, 2008*

ACTIVE/INACTIVE GANG STATUS REVIEW

CDC 128B

Appendix 3:
New Afrikan Creed

1. i believe in the spirituality, humanity and genius of [New Afrikan] people, and in our new pursuit of these values.

2. i believe in the family and the community, and in the community as a family, and i will work to make this concept live.

3. i believe in the community as more important than the individual.

4. i believe in constant struggle for freedom, to end oppression and build a better world. i believe in collective struggle; in fashioning victory in concert with my brothers and sisters.

5. i believe that the fundamental reason our oppression continues is that We, as a people, lack the power to control our lives.

6. i believe that the fundamental way to gain that power, and end oppression, is to build a sovereign [New Afrikan] nation.

7. i believe that all the land in America, upon which We have lived for a long time, which We have worked and built upon, and which We have fought to stay on, is land that belongs to us as a people.

8. i believe in the Malcolm X Doctrine: that We must organize upon this land, and hold a plebiscite, to tell the world by a vote that We are free and our land independent, and that, after the

vote, We must stand ready to defend ourselves, establishing the nation beyond contradiction.

9. Therefore, i pledge to struggle without cease, until We have won sovereignty. i pledge to struggle without fail until We have built a better condition than the world has yet known.

10. i will give my life, if that is necessary; i will give my time, my mind, my strength, and my wealth because this IS necessary.

11. i will follow my chosen leaders and help them.

12. i will love my brothers and sisters as myself.

13. i will steal nothing from a brother or sister, cheat no brother or sister, misuse no brother or sister, inform on no brother or sister, and spread no gossip.

14. i will keep myself clean in body, dress and speech, knowing that i am a light set on a hill, a true representative of what We are building.

15. i will be patient and uplifting with the deaf, dumb and blind, and i will seek by word and deed to heal the [New Afrikan] family, to bring into the Movement and into the Community mothers and fathers, brothers and sisters left by the wayside.

Now, freely and of my own will, i pledge this Creed, for the sake of freedom for my people and a better world, on pain of disgrace and banishment if i prove false. For, i am no longer deaf, dumb or blind. i am, by inspiration of the ancestors and grace of the Creator—a New Afrikan.

Appendix 4
New Afrikan
Declaration of Independence

WE, [New Afrikan] People in America, in consequence of arriving at a knowledge of ourselves as a people with dignity, long deprived of that knowledge; as a consequence of revolting with every decimal of our collective and individual beings against the oppression that for three hundred years has destroyed and broken and warped the bodies and minds and spirits of our people in America, in consequence of our raging desire to be free of this oppression, to destroy this oppression wherever it assaults _humankind_ in the world, and in consequence of inextinguishable determination to go a different way, to build a new and better world, do hereby declare ourselves forever free and independent of the jurisdiction of the United States of America and the obligations which that country's unilateral decision to make our ancestors and ourselves paper-citizens placed on us.

We claim no rights from the United States of America other than those rights belonging to human beings anywhere in the world, and these include the right to damages, reparations, due us from the grievous injuries sustained by our ancestors and ourselves by reason of United States lawlessness.

Ours is a revolution against oppression—our own oppression and that of all people in the world. And it is a revolution for a better life, a better station for _all_, a surer harmony with the forces of life in the universe. We therefore see these aims as the aims of our revolution:

→ To free [New Afrikan] people in America from oppression;

→ To support and wage the world revolution until all people everywhere are so free;

→ To build a new Society that is better than what We now know and as perfect as _We_ can make it;

→ To assure all people in the New Society maximum opportunity and equal access to that maximum;

→ To promote industriousness, responsibility, scholarship, and service;

→ To create conditions in which freedom of religion abounds and the pursuit of God and/or destiny, place and purpose of _humankind_ in the Universe will be without hindrance;

→ To build a [New Afrikan] independent nation where no sect or religious creed subverts or impedes the building of the New Society, the New State Government, or achievement of the Aims of the Revolution as set forth in this Declaration;

→ To end exploitation of _human beings_ by _each other_ or the environment;

→ To assure equality of rights for the sexes;

→ To end color and class discrimination, while not abolishing salubrious diversity, and to promote self-respect and mutual understanding among all people in the society;

→ To protect and promote the personal dignity and integrity of the individual, and _his or her_ natural rights;

→ To place the major means of production and trade in the trust of the State to assure the benefits of this earth and _our_ genius and labor to society and all its members, and

→ To encourage and reward the individual for hard work and initiative and insight and devotion to the Revolution.

_In_ mutual trust and great expectation, We the undersigned, for ourselves and for those who look to us but are unable personally to affix their signatures hereto, do join in this solemn Declaration of Independence, and to support this Declaration and to assure the success of the Revolution, We pledge without reservation ourselves, our talents, and all our worldly goods.

California Prison Struggle Links

The contents of this book were being assembled during the 2013 California prisoners' hungerstrike, which initially involved over 30,000 participants. It is impossible to include the history of this strike here. Despite the numbers involved, the death of prisoner Billy Sell, and the fact that the strike lasted from July 8 to September 5, it remains unclear what the future holds.

What us clear is that California's prisons have emerged as one of the critical fronts in the battle against genocide, and against the ruling prison State. Here are some online resources relevant to this struggle:

→ The Prisoner Hunger Strike Solidarity Coalition: prisonerhungerstrikesolidarity.wordpress.com

→ California Prison Focus: http://prisons.org

→ The Rock Newsletter: http://bit.ly/1gFT9Xk
or go to http://www.prisonart.org *and click on link on right sidebar*

→ Solitary Watch: http://solitarywatch.com

→ San Francisco Bay View: http://sfbayview.com

→ Kersplebedeb: http://kersplebedeb.com/posts/category/prisoners/california/

Note on Sources

"Monster Kody: an interview wit' author Sanyika Shakur" first appeared in the *San Francisco Bay View*, June 20, 2012.

"Who Are You?" first appeared in the *San Francisco Bay View*, February 15, 2012.

The interview "Objectively, the situation with me and these pigs is political" was conducted on January 1, 2013, by Rafiki, questions provided by Kersplebedeb.

The other essays in the book were all written in 2011 and 2012, while Sanyika was incarcerated in Pelican Bay SHU.

The New Afrikan Creed and New Afrikan Declaration of Independence were reproduced from *Crossroad* vol. 9 #4.

The Five Core Demands of the 2011 California Prisoners' Hunger Strike were taken from the website of the Prisoners' Hunger Strike Solidarity Coalition (http://prisonerhungerstrikesolidarity.wordpress.com)

Where possible, efforts have been made to contact the artists and photographers whose works illustrate this book.

KER SPL EBE DEB

Since 1998 Kersplebedeb has been an important source of radical literature and agit prop materials.

The project has a non-exclusive focus on anti-patriarchal and anti-imperialist politics, framed within an anticapitalist perspective. A special priority is given to writings regarding armed struggle in the metropole, and the continuing struggles of political prisoners and prisoners of war.

The Kersplebedeb website provides downloadable activist artwork, as well as historical and contemporary writings by revolutionary thinkers from the anarchist and communist traditions.

Kersplebedeb can be contacted at:

Kersplebedeb
CP 63560
CCCP Van Horne
Montreal, Quebec
Canada
H3W 3H8

email: info@kersplebedeb.com
web: www.kersplebedeb.com
      secure.leftwingbooks.net

Kersplebedeb

Meditations on Frantz Fanon's Wretched of the Earth

New Afrikan Revolutionary Writings
by James Yaki Sayles

"This exercise is about more than our desire to read and understand *Wretched* (as if it were about some abstract world, and not our own); it's about more than our need to understand (the failures of) the anti-colonial struggles on the African continent. This exercise is also about us, and about some of the things that We need to understand and to change in ourselves and our world."
—James Yaki Sayles [Atiba Shanna]

"Here is an authentic voice of the Black Revolution from the times of violent ghetto uprisings, re-learning the lessons of Fanon's Wretched of the Earth. Uncut, undiluted." (J. Sakai, author of Settlers: Mythology of the White Proletariat)

available from
Kersplebedeb Publishing,
CP 63560, CCCP Van Horne,
Montreal, Quebec, Canada H3W 3H8
web: leftwingtbooks.net

"When We started receiving these Meditations i was so grateful that the Comrad had taken the time to break down Wretched from a New Afrikan Communist perspective. ... It is a true weapon for Our struggle & should be read, studied, discussed, meditated upon & practiced in order to realize a better world than that in which We now live." (Sanyika Shakur)